The Really Practical Guide to Primary History

THE REALLY PRACTICAL GUIDE TO PRIMARY HISTORY

Second Edition

Margaret Wright

Stanley Thornes (Publishers) Ltd

First published in 1992 by:
Stanley Thornes (Publishers) Ltd
Ellenborough House
Wellington Street
CHELTENHAM GL50 1YW

Second edition 1996

96 97 98 99 00 / 10 9 8 7 6 5 4 3 2 1

A catalogue of this book is available from The British Library.
ISBN 0 7487 2611 X

Acknowledgements
The author and publishers are grateful to the following for permission to reproduce photographs.
Mary Evans Picture Library (page 35, top; page 36, top).

Printed and bound in Great Britain at The Bath Press, Avon

Contents

1

Understanding the NC Statutory Orders

The revision to the National Curriculum for history in 1995, after the Curriculum Review, has retained the place of history within the primary classroom. There are elements of the Revised Orders which provide continuity with 1991 planning and content, but there are also some aspects which address teachers' concerns with the earlier regulations. Familiar structures and phrases are used in the latest documents so that good practice from 1991 can be developed from September 1995 when the Orders came into force.

The framework set out in the National Curriculum guidelines gives a clear indication of the history content for ages 5–11 years, as well as the skills, concepts and understanding to be assessed within the level descriptors.

For all schools, the specified content has been reduced, especially at key stage 2. Attainment targets have been replaced by level descriptors, and a new relationship between areas of study and key elements has been set out to help planning and progression. These chapters aim to address many of the issues related to planning, approaches to learning, evaluation and assessment, in a practical way.

Content for history

The National Curriculum document for history presents two clearly separate programmes of study for key stages 1 and 2.

Key stage 1

This consists of three areas of study to be taught throughout the key stage. Within it there are five key elements for developing an awareness of the past and an understanding of the differences between past and present times:

Areas of study
1 Everyday life, work, leisure and culture in the past, progressing from the familiar to the distant in time
2 The lives of different famous men and women
3 Past events of different types

NB 2 and 3 must include examples from British History.

Key elements
1 Chronology
2 Range and depth of historical knowledge
3 Interpretations of history
4 Historical enquiry
5 Organisation and communication of historical information

Although there will be no assessment of children's communication of historical information, there is a requirement to provide opportunities for oral, visual and written presentations. How children learn about the past remains firmly in the hands of the teacher, and the wider the variety of media used the more history will be seen as an exciting and dramatic vehicle for other curriculum areas as well as a subject in its own right.

Key stage 2

The content of this key stage for National Curriculum is much more rigorous and precise than key stage 1 in terms of periods in history to be studied. There also exists a requirement to provide a balance for the history experience across political, economic, technical and scientific, social, religious, cultural and aesthetic.

The study units form the basis of history content and are statements of the minimum requirements for a teacher to cover. For each unit, there are clear instructions on what aspects of that period to study with children, but teachers must feel free to add content and expand on the units. The Orders only provide a framework within which teachers must develop their own schemes of work, suited to their pupils, school and locality.

The term 'unit' is convenient for describing areas of content to be covered and does not necessarily imply that history has to be taught as a separate block on a timetable. How the history units fit into the school's overall scheme of work is again a matter for the school to decide.

During key stage 2, over four years, all children must have experience of six units or areas of content for history.

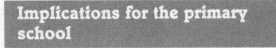

Implications for the primary school

There are again various considerations which primary schools have to think about,

---

SIX STUDY UNITS
1   Romans, Anglo-Saxons and Vikings in Britain
2   Life in Tudor Times
3a   Victorian Britain   or 3b   Britain since 1930
4   Ancient Greece
5   Local History
6   A Past Non-European Society

Across the key stage, plan to give experience of:
a)   Some aspects in outline, some in depth
b)   Aspects of the histories of England, Ireland, Scotland and Wales
c)   Various perspectives of history

---

both in devising a policy for history and also at the annual planning stage. First, some teachers will be considering history for the first time in its present form and others will be wondering how to adapt their current schemes and activities to the demands of history in the New Orders. Secondly, although there is no statutory time obligation for history, there is a general suggestion that history should occupy 36 hours per year at key stage 1 and 45 hours per year at key stage 2. Within topic work, the time allowance for any one subject area will be impossible to monitor, especially in history which involves so much language, literacy and oracy work, but teachers at least know that history still needs a reasonable slice of the curriculum cake.

Another consideration is assessment of historical skills and understanding as there is still a statutory requirement to report to parents at the end of each year on progress, even though there are no SATs in history. Planning needs to incorporate suggestions for assessing children in history, and needs to be linked to key elements.

Planning and deciding on the approach

One of the first decisions a school needs to make is the approach to the subject within their school. This may be based on existing good practice but there may need to be some adjustments to incorporate all the elements of National Curriculum Core and Foundation subjects.

Most schools will want to keep an integrated approach wherever possible but at times, especially for key stage 2, this will not be easy. The most feasible way to incorporate all the elements is through the subject-focused topics so that certain ones will have a history bias in the same way that others will have a science bias. Some existing science schemes may have a two-year cycle and it may be advisable for history and other foundation subjects to fit this pattern.

A second decision relating to approach for history concerns the order of the units at key stage 2. Although there is no requirement to arrange the units chronologically, there are many schools who will choose to do so because it provides a logical framework in a school where there are no mixed age classes and because their school philosophy dictates that approach. However, small schools with mixed age classes have always been unable to adhere to a chronological order requirement and need not feel any concern over this as there is no firm evidence to suggest that children's sense of time and its passing is improving by learning history in a chronological sequence. Introducing more opportunities to sequence and to use timelines are more valuable here. These ideas will be dealt with later in the book.

The need for a policy and scheme of work

Some schools have always had a policy statement for humanities or history which included a scheme of work, a list of content areas or relevant topics, but this has often sat on the staffroom shelf gathering dust and rarely used except when the dreaded inspector calls. The policy statement should encapsulate the ethos of the school, the approach to learning, the plans and requirements for history and the methods by which children will achieve both National Curriculum levels and the aims and objectives of the school for history. It is vital, now that governors, inspectors and parents have more access and more accountability in the learning process, that teachers state what they are doing and why as briefly as possible. The statement is a working document and should be updated frequently especially in the early years of National Curriculum when approaches and ideas may change.

A scheme of work is also vital so that teachers have an overview of the key stages from the child's viewpoint. It avoids unnecessary repetition and enables the teacher to plan for progression in content and learning activities. Both of these items of paperwork are relatively new for some primary schools. Advice should be sought from the LEA for general guidelines and from recent literature published by HMSO which contains HMI advice and opinion. A series of relevant questions to ask when writing a policy statement appears in Chapter 2.

Importance of annual planning

Whereas the scheme of work should indicate the elements of National Curriculum Programmes of Study to be covered in any one academic year, the annual planning will derive the topic headings which cover these elements and the term/half-term in which they are to be studied. At this point the teacher has some freedom left to organise 'how' the different elements of history, geography and science, etc. will be delivered in the classroom and to design activities relevant to the key elements. Building on evidence from the previous teacher, planning should vary according to the needs of the particular children that year. It may also be at this stage that visits and visitors to the classroom are arranged to avoid clashes with previous years.

Liaison across the key stages

If we are to avoid some of the pitfalls of pre-National Curriculum history, then links need to be established between infant and junior schools and between junior and secondary. Time rarely allows for meetings or discussions during the normal school day but some schools are finding ways to meet more regularly, for example:

- On INSET days
- Using INSET money to release teachers to talk and plan
- Going on joint visits, for example to visit a local feature or building with Year 6 and Year 7
- Sharing resources between the schools
- Liaising over methods, assessment and recording achievement.

Resourcing for history

History needs time, money, staffing and resources in the same way that other subjects do. Unfortunately, few of these are readily available now or in the near future. This is why it is vitally important to plan the resourcing of history so that best use is made of current expertise and stock and a priority established for future spending.

An audit is a good way of analysing what is needed. It should take account of:

- Staff specialisms and interests/personal resources
- Local speakers, helpful adults and parents
- Money available
- Existing materials in school
- Staff development needs in history
- National Curriculum minimum requirements.

The locality can be a rich source of cheap or free materials for history. It can be a starting point for refurbishing a history resource bank. Making contacts with local agencies like County Hall for maps and building plans, with Record Offices for archive material and with museums for artefacts can be very worthwhile. Local people can also be the basis for a great deal of oral history which can be taped or written in a cheaply produced pamphlet which then becomes a resource for next year. Local people and newspapers can also provide photographs and news items from the immediate past which would fit with history topics like 'Britain since the 1930s'.

Some schools, especially small rural ones, will benefit from forming a co-operative cluster which can resource the chosen topics and share them around the schools. This of course needs careful planning which brings us back to the importance of the scheme of work and annual planning, but this kind of arrangement can save time and money as ideas and INSET are shared. It can also be a very supportive framework.

The resources, once obtained, will need cataloguing and storing either by topic or some other simple classification. The library area or a small store-room would be ideal, but a well-labelled cupboard or bookshelf may be all you can hope for. An organised resources area will save such a lot of duplication and time for the busy teacher. It would also help if topic plans and other useful ideas and contacts were stored in the same place. (See later for further guidance.)

Choosing a history co-ordinator

You may be wondering who will instigate all these valuable activities for history and wave the magic wand over the school cupboard. Within each school, there should be a designated postholder for the subject, chosen by the headteacher. HMI reported in 1989 that where they saw evidence of good practice in history there had usually been a co-ordinator for the curriculum area within that school. (*Aspects of teaching and learning in history and geography in the primary school*, DES 1989.)

In some schools, history may be the only responsibility of that teacher; in small schools history may be one of several tasks. It is advisable for headteachers to choose someone with an interest or qualification in the subject but again that is not always possible. There are certain tasks which the co-ordinator should assume in the role for history, as set out here.

The role of the history co-ordinator

Short-term

- Conduct an audit of the school for history
- Devise and display action plans when necessary or school development plans
- Draw up programmes of work for discussion, manage the implementation and assess their effectiveness
- Use external expertise
- Organise and order resources so that they are relevant and accessible
- Match the curriculum with children's abilities now and update when necessary.
- Encourage assessment and recording in a variety of ways

Long-term

- Act as consultant by keeping up to date with the latest documents, learning methods, conferences and courses available.
- Lead working parties and subject groups, either in the school, cluster or county
- Organise workshop sessions for colleagues
- Work alongside colleagues to develop history learning activities and improve their confidence
- Monitor progression

Summary

School history has moved into a five-year period of stability. The main challenge for change is firmly in the hands of the primary teachers. Careful and co-operative planning can lead to exciting and informative learning activities both at key stages 1 and 2.

How do we achieve success without insanity?

Work systematically with the following targets in mind:

- Careful discussion of policy and planning
- Cluster with other schools for survival and support
- Cultivate links across key stages
- Compile and catalogue resources over a period of time.

The advice in the next five chapters relates directly to these targets for managing primary history.

2

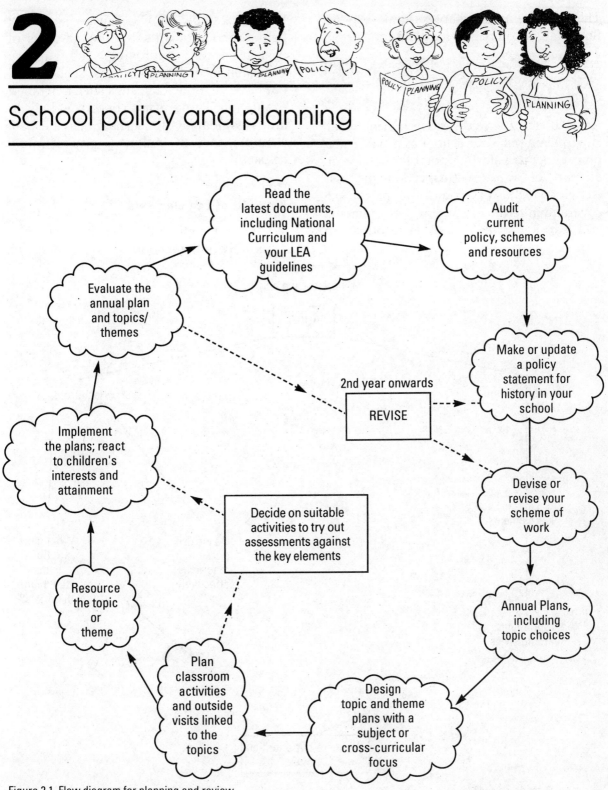

School policy and planning

Read the latest documents, including National Curriculum and your LEA guidelines

Audit current policy, schemes and resources

Evaluate the annual plan and topics/themes

Make or update a policy statement for history in your school

2nd year onwards

REVISE

Implement the plans; react to children's interests and attainment

Devise or revise your scheme of work

Decide on suitable activities to try out assessments against the key elements

Resource the topic or theme

Annual Plans, including topic choices

Plan classroom activities and outside visits linked to the topics

Design topic and theme plans with a subject or cross-curricular focus

Figure 2.1 Flow diagram for planning and review

The guidance in this chapter is linked to the flow diagram on page 7 for planning.

on page 7

Where do we start? Audit activities and their purpose

An audit activity involves considering what is happening in your school at a particular time, either as a starting point for change or as part of a review/inspection process. Activities for history could look at current coverage in terms of content, key elements and learning styles or look at resources in terms of human and material.

Figure 2.2 shows how a full review could help a school towards deciding an order of priorities for improving the history provision in their school. Most schools will not have the time to arrange such a detailed evaluation. If the major concern is how to link key elements to learning activities, for example, then the following process might be useful.

An audit of key elements

- Choose a topic which has been covered recently in the school.

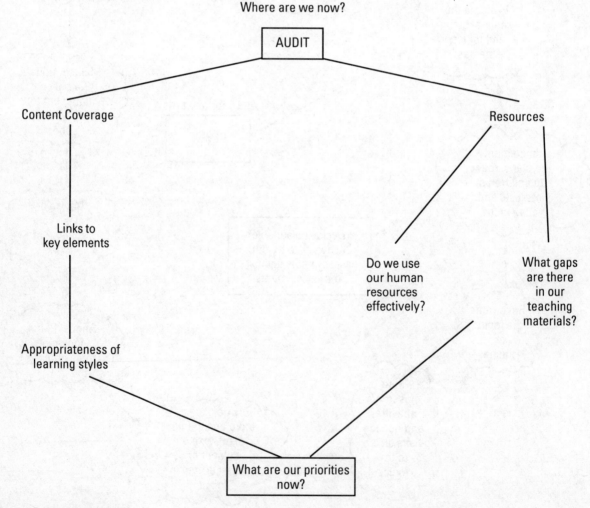

Figure 2.2 What do we audit?

8

Key element	Key stage 1	Key stage 2
1 Chronology	1 • Sequencing of objects and events • Using the language of time	1 • Placing events, people and changes in a chronological framework • Using dates and time language as well as terms that define periods
2 Range and depth of historical knowledge and understanding	2 • Hearing stories • Recognising 'cause and effect' • Identifying differences	2 • Learning about features of periods and societies, attitudes and experiences • Explaining reasons for and results of historical aspects studied • Describing and making links
3 Interpretations	3 Identifying different ways the past is shown	3 Identifying and explaining reasons for different interpretations and representations
4 Historical enquiry	4 • Looking at different sources • Asking and answering questions	4 • Finding out from a range of sources • Asking and answering questions; selecting and recording relevant detail
5 Organisation and communication	5 Telling, drawing and writing history	5 • Recalling information, including dates and terms • Using the relevant historical language in communicating • Using a variety of ways to retell history

Figure 2.3 Key elements for key stage 1 and key stage 2

- List what you and the children did in the left-hand column (activities).

- In the right-hand column (key elements) write in the skills or concepts covered by each learning activity.

- When complete, analyse the result in terms of:
  a) coverage of key elements
  b) level descriptors for your key stage
  c) identifying gaps.

- Discuss whether and how you would alter the topic so that it meets the needs of your children and National Curriculum. For example, by adding new activities or extending existing ones, by making the materials more demanding or by providing a wider range of sources.

Figure 2.4 may help you.

TOPIC: A LOCAL STUDY LINKED TO THE ROMANS IN BRITAIN	
Activities	Key elements
1 Visit to Corinium museum, Cirencester. Filling in a worksheet and discussing the Roman way of life	Historical enquiry
2 Using the recorded findings from the visit to write about the differences between Roman homes then and now	Organisation and communication

Figure 2.4

An audit of resources

Choose one of the study units for history, for example Life in Tudor Times, and list the learning activities you would like to organise for the term or half-term. Next, list the resources you will need for those activities in terms of supervision, books, pictures, other historical sources, equipment, etc. In a third column, tick the resources you already have and leave blank the resources you require (Figure 2.5). The next step is to find out where you might acquire those resources. Before buying, you might try colleagues in other schools or a local resource centre so that costs are kept to a minimum.

Activities	Resources needed	Audit of resources
1 Comparing pictures of Tudor and modern homes: interior & exterior	Sets of pictures, posters and reference books	
2 Investigating life in a Tudor household - rich and poor		Only a few. Buy more and try the School Library Loan Service

Figure 2.5

List the items you need to buy and establish a priority for purchasing these. You may wish to write into your policy statement a commitment to resource history over the next few years as part of your school development plan.

An audit activity is a useful preparation for writing a policy statement because it gives you an idea of what is going on in school at the moment and allows you to build on good practice for the future as well as identifying areas for improvement or change.

Writing a policy statement for history

National Curriculum in history should build on existing methods and strategies in your school and the policy statement should incorporate previous aims and objectives which the school considers important. Every school's statement will be different but the guidance here gives a framework for compiling a brief, but useful, document which can be revised and up-dated as National Curriculum progresses and as the needs of the school change. It will form the basis and philosophy for planning and therefore should be discussed and decided initially before planning a scheme of work and topics.

The following questions could be used as part of an INSET day or staff meeting to promote discussion on policy in history. The answers can be streamlined to form your policy statement.

Questions to ask yourself and your colleagues

1 Why do we need a policy ?
   The answers to this may include the LEA policy and guidelines, the need for a coherent approach and purpose to planning, the necessity of informing teachers, newly qualified teachers, students, governors, parents and inspectors.

2 What has been the policy prior to this date and how will it change with or integrate the requirements of National Curriculum, for example?
   Schools which are writing a policy for the first time may not need to answer this question.

3 What are your general aims in history? (This may include developing certain

attitudes and may link with other humanities subjects.)

4 What are your objectives? What concepts are you developing in the school?

For example:

- A sense of time, chronology
- Cause and effect
- Similarity and difference
- Understanding interpretations of history.

You may include reference to the National Curriculum key elements here.

5 How will you develop the concepts and skills in history, at what age and by what strategies? (See Figure 2.6)

| Concepts for history | Ideas for developing these at | |
	Key stage 1	Key stage 2
Chronological understanding	Sequencing pictures and objects Making simple timelines	Use Study Unit One, Romans, Anglo-Saxons and Vikings in Britain, to look at changes over time Produce a detailed timeline
Similarity and difference	Compare pictures and photographs from 'then' and 'now'	In a local study, find evidence of similarity and difference in pictures and maps, either between Victorians and now or over a long time period

Figure 2.6

6 How does history contribute to the rest of the curriculum?
Here, you should include how history can play a vital role in developing general skills of enquiry and observation as well as social skills. Also link your history content to other core subjects such as science and languages as well as geography and cross-curricular areas – for example, multicultural awareness, economic and industrial understanding, equal opportunities. You will find that history is a good vehicle for dealing with many curriculum requirements.

7 What particular teaching and learning strategies will you be encouraging for history?
This should include reference to the organisation of your scheme of work. For example, will it be a two or three-year cycle in each key stage to ensure coverage of National Curriculum content. You need to list the kind of activities you wish to promote in the classroom, for example, an enquiry approach, use of role-play, handling artefacts, how children should communicate their historical findings in a variety of ways. The scheme of work could be attached to the policy statement for easy reference.

8 How will you be assessing the children for history? How often will you plan this and how will you record the results?
Your answers here should link to school policy generally and to LEA guidelines. Amongst assessment of core subjects, history may have a less significant place, but although there are no SATs, reporting of the National Curriculum attainment level at the end of the key stage is still being considered.

9 Who will be responsible for history in the school?
In small schools, the role of history co-ordinator may be a combined one with other subject responsibility. However, there needs to be a postholder since certain tasks exist for the subject and its development, for example, INSET and resourcing. Any comments here should also be linked to job descriptions in the

school staff development policy. (See page 5 on the role of the History Co-ordinator in Chapter 1.)

10 What resources are available for history? This section is not intended as a list of resources but as a statement of the nature of resources for history, where and how they are organised and by whom. If there is a special resources room, who has access and who has responsibility for buying new resources? Human resources, such as parental help and specialisms could also be noted here.

11 What are your plans for cross-phase links, for example, pre-school and key stage 3? Will you discuss your schemes with them?

12 What is your school policy on visits and safety during fieldwork?
Teachers need to know the requirements before they start to plan. Elsewhere you may wish to make a list of useful places to visit, linked to National Curriculum units.

13 How will you evaluate the policy and scheme of work in history?
You will need to plan for short-term evaluation, for example, at the end of the year and also an in-depth evaluation which you may wish to link to an inspection. You would want to incorporate any plans here in your school development plan.

Planning a scheme of work for key stage 1 and 2

You will have made a policy decision about whether your approach to history in the school will be within a cross-curricular framework through topics or by a single subject route. In most primary schools, the topic approach will still be popular and appropriate. There are various ways to approach the planning. Generally, it is now advisable to start with the elements of the programmes of study which need to be covered and to set these out in a basic scheme for each key stage so that individual teachers are aware of their responsibilities. From this basic scheme, annual planning can derive topic headings for various elements which link together. Sections of the programme of study which do not easily fit the topic can be dealt with occasionally in a mini-topic.

A key stage 1 scheme of work For key stage 1 the basic scheme of work, after using the three areas of study, might look like this:

Year group	Elements of the Programme of Study to be covered
Reception	Personal timelines – stories and photographs Toys then and now, handling artefacts A story from a past culture
Year one	Family life within living memory } Using Christmas then and now } artefacts Stories from various cultures Comparing work and homes since 1945 A local study – evidence in the locality Stories about famous people Victorian life

Year two	Shopping then and now
	Transport since 1945
	Life in the fifties and sixties
	  – handling artefacts
	An ancient society, eg Ancient Egypt
	  – including famous people
	A global celebration,
	  eg Chinese New Year
	A museum visit

Figure 2.7 Exemplar key stage 1

Annual planning might then produce a topic plan for one year as shown in the table opposite.

Reception	**Settling in** **Language work**	TOYS AND CHRISTMAS	OURSELVES Personal timelines and family Handling photos then and now	GROWTH Story about a young Viking boy	**Science led topic**
Year one	VICTORIANS • handling artefacts • visit a Victorian schoolroom or classroom roleplay	CHRISTMAS THEN AND NOW Victorian or Medieval	FAMILY AND HOMES – within living memory – using artefacts	PEOPLE WHO HELP US (in history go back to 1945)	THE LOCAL AREA • looking at evidence • important local people
Year two	SHOPPING these now link to maths, design and language	**Science led topic**	Chinese New Year – a short global celebration	CHANGES Life in the fifties and sixties, compared with now	SHAPE • Ancient Egyptians • Story about Tutankhamen • A museum visit	MOVEMENT Transport since 1945 linked to science, Technology and Geography

Figure 2.8 Exemplar key stage 1 Annual Plan linking history with other subject areas in topics

Most of the above topic headings are adaptable enough to allow history to be linked with other subject areas. Some have a starting point in history or a focus in comparing then and now. Throughout the key stage stories can be used as starting points for mini-topics but these can be more spontaneous choices as long as a record is kept and other teachers know which stories are being used.

Annual planning will also need to specify which topics are most suited to the various sources of history mentioned in the National Curriculum Document (page 13), DES 1991.

For example:

Artefacts
The Victorians
Life since 1930
Family objects and photos
For ancient cultures there may be reproductions available from museum visits

Pictures and photographs
One or other will be available for most topics

Music
Use songs with infants or simple ways of making sounds relevant to the time. There will be more songs available for more recent history.

Adults talking
Use parents, teachers and locals. Ask adults to be involved in role-play for more distant time periods.

Written sources
Use books, stories, diary extracts, news items and simple archive evidence.

Buildings and sites
Start with the familiar sites such as homes and local buildings. Transfer these ideas on visits to another locality or to a castle or museum.

Computer-based material
Use simple database programmes to record evidence for other children to research, for example, 'Our facts' for recording details of local buildings.

All topics should encourage an enquiry approach and should allow children to develop a variety of reporting and communication skills. For infants there is a requirement for children to show their understanding visually, orally and in writing.

A key stage 2 scheme of work At key stage 2, the history provision seems much more restrictive, but unless schools wish to teach in a separate subject way there is still a great deal of scope for a cross-curricular approach. One of the major hurdles is the amount to be covered for the core National Curriculum subjects which leaves the foundation subjects, like history, in a squeezed situation. One way of fitting all the elements of the programmes of study into a scheme of work is to take the content-dominated ones like geography, science and history and to make cards containing the main elements to be covered in the key stage. See Figure 2.9.

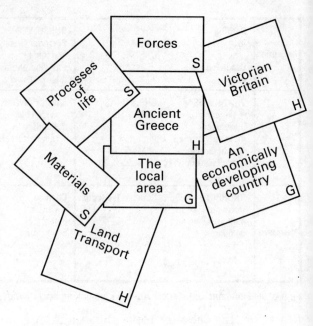

Figure 2.9 Key stage 2: Curriculum Planning Map

GROUP	TERM 1	TERM 2	TERM 3
YEAR THREE			Ancient Times for History GREECE | Geography
YEAR FOUR	CHANGE | Romans, Anglo-Saxons and Vikings in Britain (focus on Romans)		
YEAR FIVE		Life in Tudor Times HOMES AND HEALTH ／＼ Science　　Language	A study of the town through a long period THE LOCALITY ／|＼ Geography | Science Technology
YEAR SIX **OR 4-YEAR CYCLE**		THE VICTORIANS	Non-European Society in the Past EGYPT | Geography

NB The blank spaces are for Science led topics.

Figure 2.10 Key stage 2: An exemplar scheme

14

Plan out a large grid as in Figure 2.10 or 2.11 (to go on the floor or a table) and spend some time moving the cards around to see how any link together or remain separate topics.

The history units do not have to be taught in chronological order but some junior schools, which are large enough to have single-age classes, may prefer to teach in this way. Their scheme might look like Figure 2.10.

Many schools have mixed age classes and will be working towards a scheme with a two-, three- or four-year cycle for their main topics. History will also fit this approach as in Figure 2.11.

In some schools there may be children who stay in one class for three years and then jump a class for Year 6. If it is impossible to organise numbers of children to suit a two- or three-year cycle, it may be that for a few children they will be repeating some periods of history or missing them altogether. Two possible solutions might be:

1 If children are likely to repeat the Victorians topic, change the main focus of the topic second time around and allow some small group work on different aspects of Victorian Britain in your annual planning. The same principle applies to other periods of history.

2 Alternatively, a group of children could be directed to work on group or individual research on the period they have not

	GROUP	TERM 1		TERM 2	TERM 3	
7–9 year-olds	1st year of cycle	Ancient Greece	↑ Ships and seafarers	Romans, Anglo-Saxons and Vikings in Britain		↑ The local study
	2nd year of the cycle	The Victorians				
9–11 year-olds	1st year of the cycle	Non-European Society in the Past		Tudors		
	2nd year of cycle	Life since the 1930s	↓			↓

Figure 2.11 Key stage 2: A 2 year cycle. Curriculum planning in history for mixed-age classes

studied and to report back to each other and the class through display or presentations.

The curriculum map, as in the models, could be the basis of the scheme of work for history at key stage 2. Some examples of ideas for annual planning and deciding topics are shown in the topic matrix. The scheme of work should also indicate the approaches to learning you wish to encourage in your school and the ways in which progression will be fostered. As with the key stage 1 scheme, you need to consider

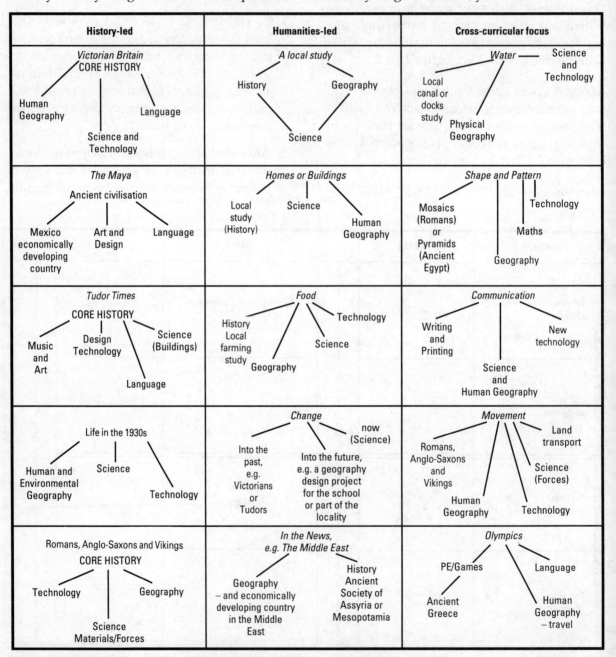

Figure 2.12 A topic matrix for key stage 2 on subject-led or cross-curricular potential

16

where certain sources for history would be most appropriate. For example, a site visit to a Mayan Temple or Egyptian Pyramid is unlikely but you would want to consider these ancient cultures from the point of view of evidence which exists today and also the gaps in evidence about these societies as well. Music as a source for history is more available for Victorian life than for Anglo-Saxon, so this needs to be incorporated in your planning. Wherever possible, build in the use of computer-based material as it becomes available or try to produce your own using hardware such as the Concept Keyboard and related packages.

Again, the general approach to history should be through enquiry and investigation, and the varied media for communication need to be encouraged throughout the key stage.

For example:
- Informed role-play/drama
- Visual display/presentation
- Narrative accounts
- Oral responses to questions
- Computer databases.

The final scheme of work which you produce should indicate which approaches are to be used and how these might link with the requirements for assessment, the attainment targets for National Curriculum.

Topic planning

The third stage of planning is that of designing the term or half-term's activities.

TOPIC TITLE: Teddy bears and toys   KSI

Key ideas, concepts or questions	Activities	Key elements	Resources
1 How long have we had teddy bears?	Looking at pictures of teddy bears and who they belonged to using 'time' vocabulary	Chronology	Teddy bears Pictures, postcards
2 How were bears made 'then' and 'now'	Comparing pictures and artefacts, visit a museum or toy hospital	Historical understanding of 'difference'	Pictures Bears museum/hospital Examples of materials
3 Sequencing pictures of bears or toys	Sequencing* activity using a simple timeline	Chronology	Pictures of bears or toys
4 Toys 'then' and 'now'	Listening to visitors talking about their favourite toys and how toys have changed or stayed the same Why do we have different favourites?	Historical understanding	Visitors Examples of Tape recorder
5	Add your own ideas here		
6			
*an activity which you may use for assessment			

Figure 2.13 A model for topic planning

This is usually the task of the individual teacher, based on decisions already made as a school for policy and the scheme of work. There are various ways to plan a topic depending on the focus, its breadth and the starting point. Here are a few examples for history and some general guidelines:

Steps to planning

- Decide on the topic/theme and the subject focus, for example, history

- Look at current good practice in your school, for example, previous topic plans
- Consult National Curriculum documents and other guidance, for example, LEA
- Spend ten minutes producing an initial topic web for all areas to be covered
- Look at the history now in detail and choose about five to seven key ideas for a half-term or eight to ten for a full term. Key ideas could be 'How were children's lives different in 1939?' or 'How useful is

TOPIC TITLE: Life since the 1930s   KS2

Key ideas, concepts or questions	Activities	Key elements	Resources
1 How did it feel to be evacuated?	Role play experience after listening to a story and watching Landmarks children at war.	Historical knowledge	Landmarks TV Broadcasts. Reference books, e.g. Tressell publication *'What was it like for children?'*
2 How were families affected by the war?	Group work to research on different aspects of the war at home; make a presentation of findings.*	Historical understanding of 'results' Communicating	Good selection of materials at a variety of levels Adults to interview
3 Life and work changed after the war	Discussing pictures of life and work since 1950s. Making a wall display of changes. Thinking about cultural and religious changes.	Understanding of 'results' and 'changes'	Various large pictures including local archive material and news items. Reference materials
4 Leisure then and now	Interview parents and grandparents Hold a 'fifties' or 'sixties' day at school Have new ideas been brought with our multicultural society?	Enquiry and understanding of change	Records/music from 1950s or 1960s. Photographs Reference books Artefacts.
5 How technology and science have changed *an activity which you may use for assessment	Individual or pairwork on various scientific developments, e.g. Space exploration Domestic equipment. Produce a booklet.	Enquiry and recording	Reference material

Figure 2.14 A model for topic planning

the 1851 census for finding out about what life was like then?'

- List the key ideas but link them to the requirements in your policy and National Curriculum. See Figure 2.14.
- Once you have the key ideas, think about the levels you are working towards in the key elements and also any general skills. Decide which activities you need to pre-pare to motivate the children, to give variety and to meet those requirements. State the key elements and finally list the resources you need for each activity.
- Across the key stage you will need as a school to make sure that your topic plans when combined give an adequate balance of political, economic, social, religious and cultural history. At the same time, consider plans for ethnic diversity and opportunities to address gender

issues. This will have been part of your policy statement and will be picked up again on evaluating topic plans.

- You may find that some topics lend themselves to different interpretations of history and others do not. There is no requirement to cover all the key elements in each topic. You will find that many arise naturally out of good practice. Plan for number 3, Interpretations of history, where possible, for example Life in Tudor Times.

Topic plans produced on the grids as in the models are not a replacement for the topic web but an extension of it, ensuring variety, coverage of statutory content and providing a teacher record of classroom activities to evaluate and use again.

3

Classroom activities for key stage 1

This chapter will concentrate on describing activities which combine elements of the programme of study and the key elements to give some ideas for classroom practice which are transferable from one period of the past to another. With younger children, the closer the link to their own experience, the more successful the activity will be. Therefore, wherever possible, hands-on activities should be tried.

Using story

History is best understood through a series of planned experiences including stories, role-play, varied observations and handling sessions. The first of these elements is picked up by National Curriculum documents and teachers are directed to give children experience of

"*myths and legends, stories about historical events, eye-witness accounts of historical events and fictional stories set in the past.*"

(*History in the National Curriculum*, HMSO 1991, page 13)

Within the key element descriptors, story is identified as a learning tool to study aspects of the past from different cultures and periods.

Stories are also provided by eye-witnesses to events in the past. For key element 3, stories can give children different interpretations of history.

Stories for children provide a framework for ordering their experiences. The 'who' and 'why' of history can be filled in through narrative by linking to real or fictional characters. HMI suggest that story and narrative are:

"*a natural way in which sequence, causation and change can be explored*"

and

"*provide a vehicle for developing language, a chronological sense, environmental understanding...*"

(*History from 5 to 16*, HMSO, page 17)

with young children. Difficult situations and conflicts can be dealt with through stories set in another time. The customs and attitudes of people in the past are often hard to assimilate if dealt with out of context. The story actually helps children to give meaning to experiences and new vocabulary and allows historical information to be transmitted in an enjoyable and digestible form.

There are various ways of using story in the classroom. The first method described here is using picture story books as a planning tool which links aspects of the areas of study and key elements. Many books available for key stage 1 can be used in this way. Most books for young children contain an element of learning about time and the sequence of events and there are plenty which directly relate to 'family life within living memory'.

Three examples follow:

- *Jack's Basket*
- *The Old Bear*
- *Grandma's Bill*

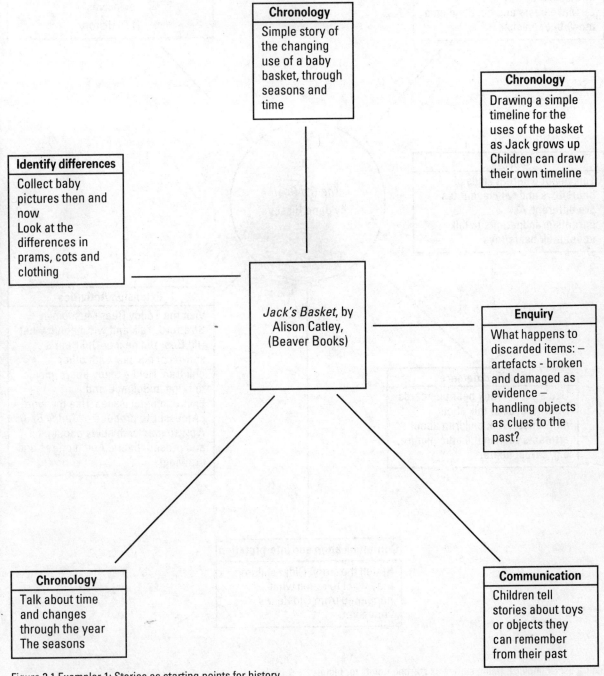

Chronology
Simple story of the changing use of a baby basket, through seasons and time

Chronology
Drawing a simple timeline for the uses of the basket as Jack grows up Children can draw their own timeline

Identify differences
Collect baby pictures then and now
Look at the differences in prams, cots and clothing

Jack's Basket, by Alison Catley, (Beaver Books)

Enquiry
What happens to discarded items: – artefacts - broken and damaged as evidence – handling objects as clues to the past?

Chronology
Talk about time and changes through the year
The seasons

Communication
Children tell stories about toys or objects they can remember from their past

Figure 3.1 Exemplar 1: Stories as starting points for history

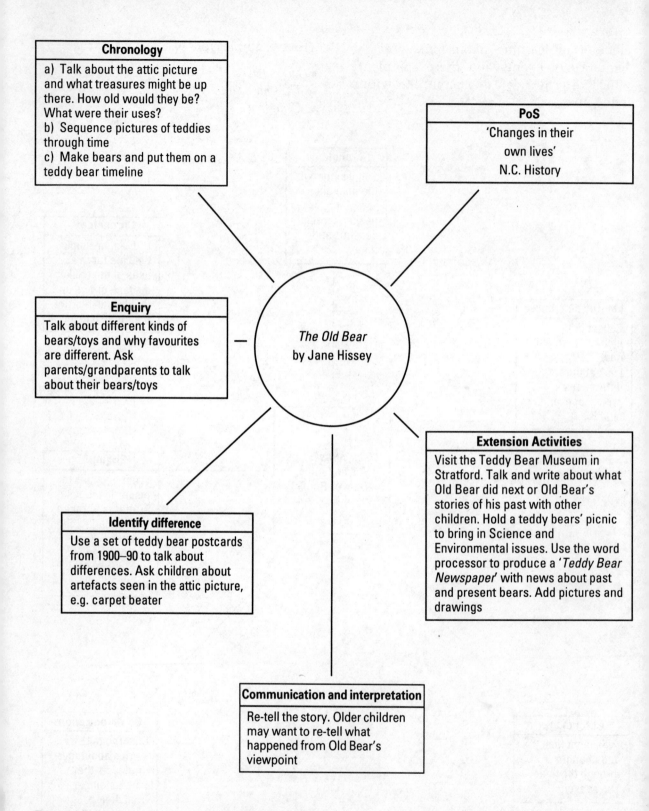

Chronology

a) Talk about the attic picture and what treasures might be up there. How old would they be? What were their uses?
b) Sequence pictures of teddies through time
c) Make bears and put them on a teddy bear timeline

PoS

'Changes in their
own lives'
N.C. History

Enquiry

Talk about different kinds of bears/toys and why favourites are different. Ask parents/grandparents to talk about their bears/toys

The Old Bear
by Jane Hissey

Identify difference

Use a set of teddy bear postcards from 1900–90 to talk about differences. Ask children about artefacts seen in the attic picture, e.g. carpet beater

Extension Activities

Visit the Teddy Bear Museum in Stratford. Talk and write about what Old Bear did next or Old Bear's stories of his past with other children. Hold a teddy bears' picnic to bring in Science and Environmental issues. Use the word processor to produce a '*Teddy Bear Newspaper*' with news about past and present bears. Add pictures and drawings

Communication and interpretation

Re-tell the story. Older children may want to re-tell what happened from Old Bear's viewpoint

Figure 3.2 Exemplar 2: Using stories as starting points for history

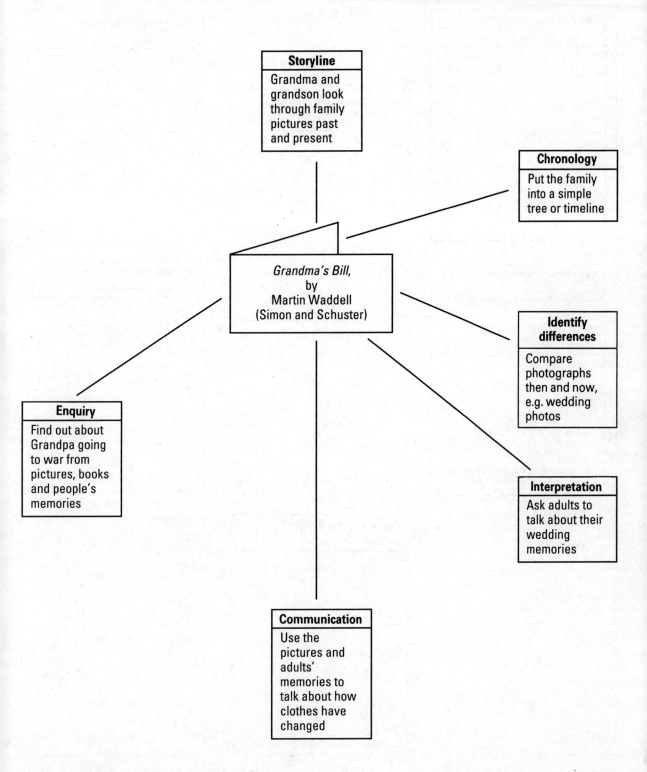

Storyline
Grandma and grandson look through family pictures past and present

Chronology
Put the family into a simple tree or timeline

Grandma's Bill,
by
Martin Waddell
(Simon and Schuster)

Identify differences
Compare photographs then and now, e.g. wedding photos

Enquiry
Find out about Grandpa going to war from pictures, books and people's memories

Interpretation
Ask adults to talk about their wedding memories

Communication
Use the pictures and adults' memories to talk about how clothes have changed

Figure 3.3 Exemplar 3: Using stories as starting points

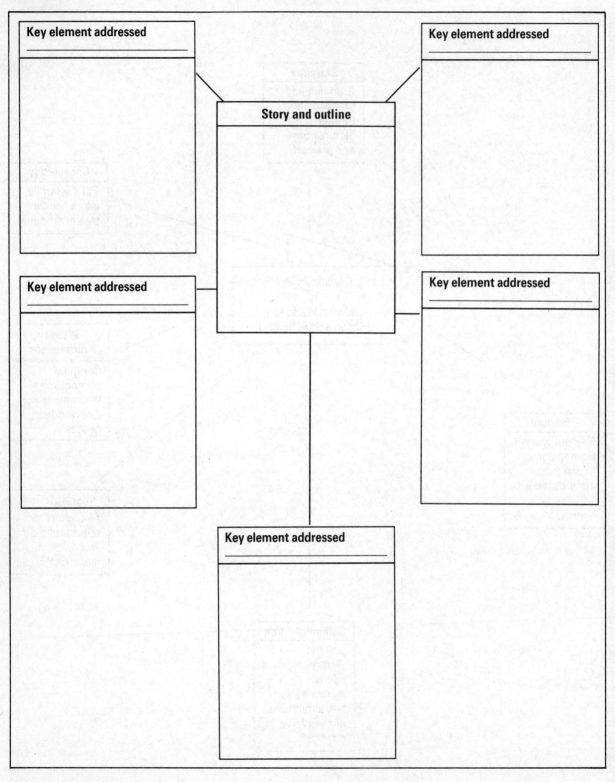

Figure 3.4 Blank grid for linking a story with activities and key elements

Famous person
When did they live (e.g. Victorian Britain)?
Main points for the story (Teacher needs to research these)
Interesting starting point for telling the story:

Figure 3.5 Grid for story planning: Key stage 1

The blank proforma (Figure 3.4 page 24) can be photocopied and used for planning work around your own favourite stories. Some books are more suitable than others for meeting certain objectives.

As well as stories as starting points, there is another element of the programme of study which can be dealt with through story-telling. This element consists of the lives of famous men and women. Biographies exist for many famous people but not necessarily in a form you would want to use with infants, with a few notable exceptions such as *Francis Drake* by Roy Gerrard (Gollancz, 1989). You may have to plan your own story after doing some research. Many of the biographical details for famous people would make tedious listening for young children. You need to pick characters which would interest them or link with their current topic or people who are in the news or being commemorated. A story planning grid is provided on page 25 (Figure 3.5) for you to photocopy. The idea is that you pick out the most important aspects of the characters' life or an interesting episode and to add a gripping starting point for your story-telling. This may be an object you are holding connected to the person, an exciting statement, a question or a picture, but the children's imagination needs to be engaged.

Similarly, stories about past events such as the Gunpowder Plot or the locality at harvest time need a specific focus. Hinging the story on a character or a particular family gives the children a framework they understand. Local people can be used to tell their own stories, as happens in Bromsberrow School, Gloucestershire, where Jean Alma talks to grandparents and records their memories as booklets which can be re-used.

Jean Alma begins Mrs Goodchild's story with a brief introduction:

'Carl's Nan, Mrs Goodchild, lived in London when she was a girl, at Woolwich, on the River Thames. Her life was very different from those who lived in the country districts. This is her story...'

'In 1938, we lived in an upstairs flat. Another family lived downstairs. We had our own front door...'

and so on. The story provides an authentic and engaging route into the past. Grandparents, as story-tellers, also provide an opportunity for developing a sense of time and generations, especially if the story begins with 'When I was six years old like you ...'

Fictional stories set in an historical context also have value in the classroom. An on-going story told in stages over a few weeks may be the link between history activities from day to day or week to week. For example, an Ancient Egyptians topic could start in the present with a boy or girl on holiday in Egypt, finding a magic charm (for example, a scarab beetle). The object (the charm) is the time key to unlocking aspects of life in Ancient Egypt, and although the child and her exploits are fictitious, the story-teller can introduce relevant vocabulary and situations from what we know of the past, over a few sessions. The story need only last five or ten minutes before children move on to various other activities related to the topic, but the thread keeps going through the work and allows the teacher to repeat relevant historical information, to question children on what they remember and to introduce new areas in each episode of the story. The children may then write their own stories as a result. I remember one story I told in an infant classroom, where I handed round a reproduction charm used for medicinal purposes in Ancient Egypt and told a simple

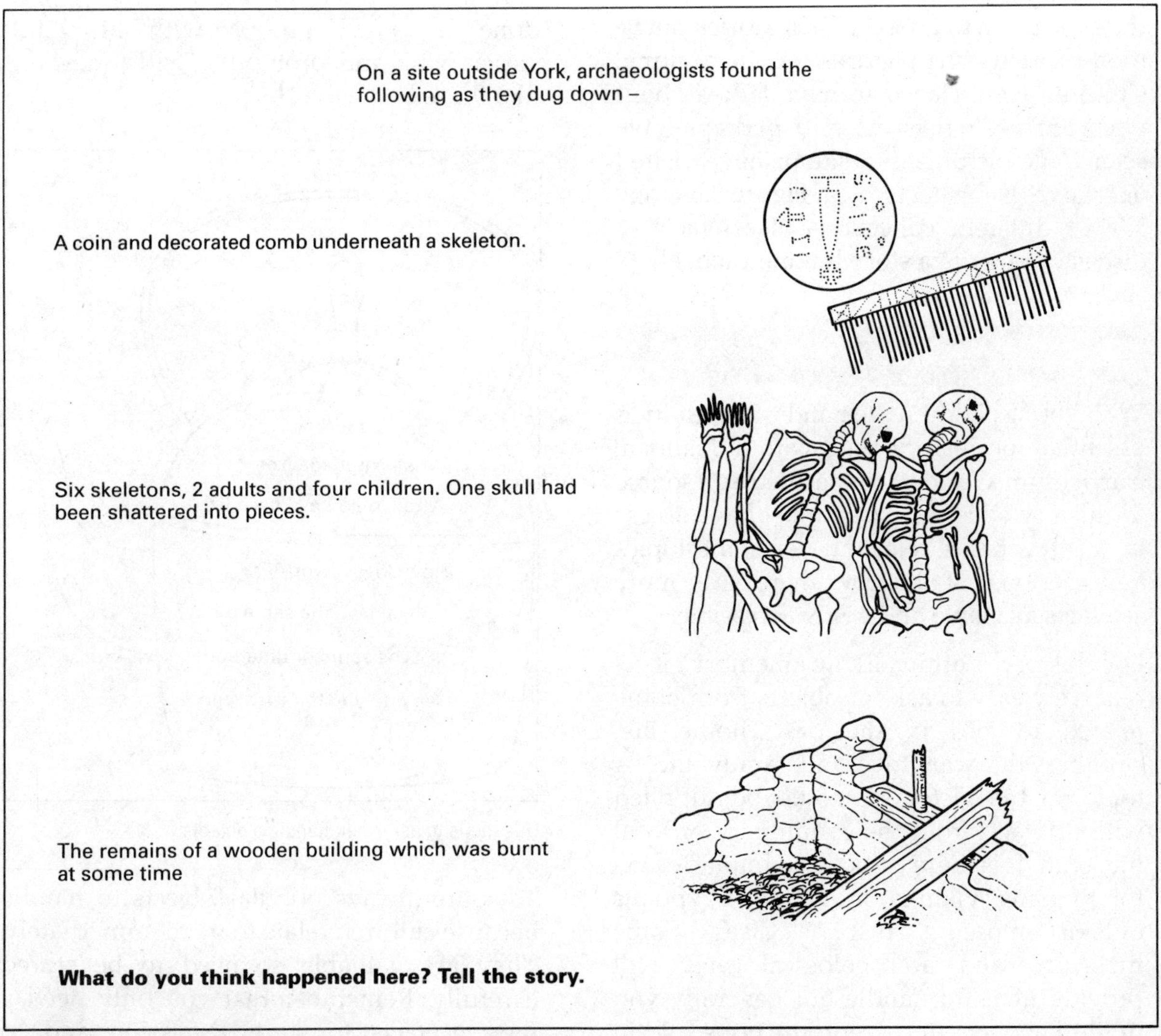

On a site outside York, archaeologists found the following as they dug down –

A coin and decorated comb underneath a skeleton.

Six skeletons, 2 adults and four children. One skull had been shattered into pieces.

The remains of a wooden building which was burnt at some time

What do you think happened here? Tell the story.

Figure 3.6 The starting point for group stories on evidence. Why are the stories different?

story based on that. One boy kept hold of the charm (a cardboard replica) for the afternoon and when I packed up to go, rushed to me with it and said 'I feel much better now!' There is a certain power in story-telling which teachers can exploit for history.

Artefacts and archaeological evidence always need interpretation to put them into context. Children can do this at a simple level and at the same time this could start discussion of different interpretations. For the activity suggested here you need to divide the children in to groups. Their stories can be retold orally, in pictures or in writing. Children would need to have talked about what archaeologists do, and perhaps have seen some pictures of a site or have visited one. Give them sheets, as in Figure 3.6 (page 27), or different collections of artefacts to discuss and write a story linking them all.

Handling artefacts

With young children the hands-on activity is essential for history and within National Curriculum. Objects are specified as a source for history which children must have access to wherever it is relevant. For some topics and periods of history there are more artefacts available and easily accessible.

For history within living memory it is relatively easy to ask for objects from home related to jobs in the past, home life, clothing, the war, toys and family life. A topic on the Victorians could be supplied with artefacts from the community or local museum. It is more difficult to find artefacts for Romans, Vikings or Ancient Egyptians outside museum display cases. Some museums and archaeological sites will provide items to handle but generally you might have to rely on reproductions sold in museum shops, for example Roman coins

from Corinium Museum, Cirencester and Viking items from Jorvik Museum, York. These can be expensive, so before you go out to buy, ask the local community, another school or your advisory service for items which you might borrow. There may be someone in your locality with a private collection they wish to show.

Respect

Before handling objects from the past, children should know that these are precious and valuable. They need to be handled and stored carefully. If the children handle the objects themselves, this is best done in small groups with an adult supervising and prompting with questions like those below.

What is it for?

What is it made from?

Who would have used it?

How does it work?

Do we have the same today?

Is it the same or different?

Why do you think it's still here?

Questions to ask when handling objects

Toys are always popular objects to handle because children relate to them immediately. They are valuable so need to be stored carefully. Remember that you only need a few artefacts to start discussion and to interest a whole class.

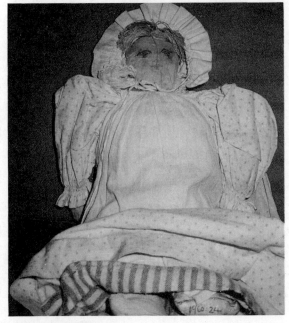

A table of objects to handle

Toys In the Past

This is made of wood and metal it makes a ringing noise

Toys In the present this is made of plastic. it makes a noise if you speak into it

David Age 6

Toys then and now

Communicating findings from objects

Children can draw the objects carefully and either describe them orally or write a little about them. A 'then' and 'now' picture helps to develop an understanding of difference. See 'Toys then and now' on the previous page. *chronology*

When children are handling objects on the classroom display table, the teacher can listen for interesting comments made and questions asked and can note these afterwards.

Role-play is another way for children to communicate their understanding and this can be organised by changing the home corner to suit the historical context. For example:

- A Victorian Kitchen
- A 1950s wash-day
- A medieval castle
- A stone-age cave
- A Roman kitchen.

Look at the diagrams below for ideas.

Role-play in a Victorian home corner

The home corner as a Roman kitchen

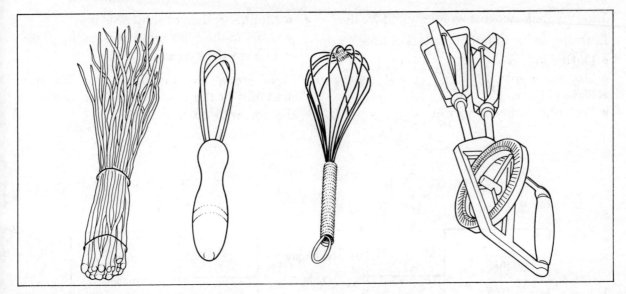

Kitchen whisks set out in an historical sequence

Artefacts can be made or borrowed for the role-play, cardboard boxes are very useful for construction and with older infants they can research and create the room themselves.

Sequencing objects can be used as well to assess children on their chronological understanding. Some museums actually have a box of objects for this purpose. After a handling session, children could look at three or four objects used for the same purpose in history and in the present to try to put them in order. A kitchen utensil is a good choice, as shown in the illustration above.

These items could be left in the classroom on display and the teacher could work round the group systematically, asking different children to sequence the objects. In this way an assessment activity becomes an integral part of the handling experience.

Oral history

Oral history and memories have been mentioned in the section on stories but it is also important to build in opportunities for children to ask questions of a variety of people, for example:

- Visitors to the classroom
- Other teachers
- Yourself
- Their parents, grandparents and other adults around them.

This way they build up a link with the recent past and also begin to grasp the different interpretations of history. They also begin to realise that evidence can be acquired from people as well as objects and sites.

Before anyone visits the classroom, children should have been prepared by deciding what you want them to find out, what questions need to be asked and how they are going to record the answers. Sometimes a tape recorder is useful.

Time activities

Many of the activities you set up for infants in history will be connected to developing a sense of time.

Time vocabulary: what words should we use?

Learning about different aspects of time:

- During the day
- Day and night
- Days of the week
- Yesterday today tomorrow
- Months of the year and seasons
- Years in their life going back in the past
- Life since they were born.

Here are a few practical ideas for time activities in the classroom which link with the demands of chronology.

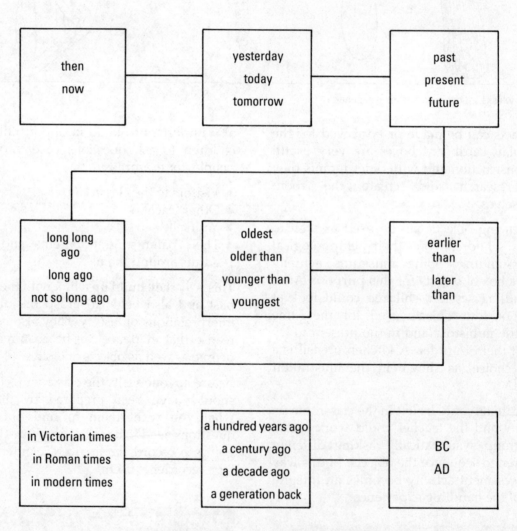

Using these terms helps children to understand them.

Figure 3.7 What words do we use for time?

Comparing then and now with pictures or photographs

Then	Say or write

Now	Say or write
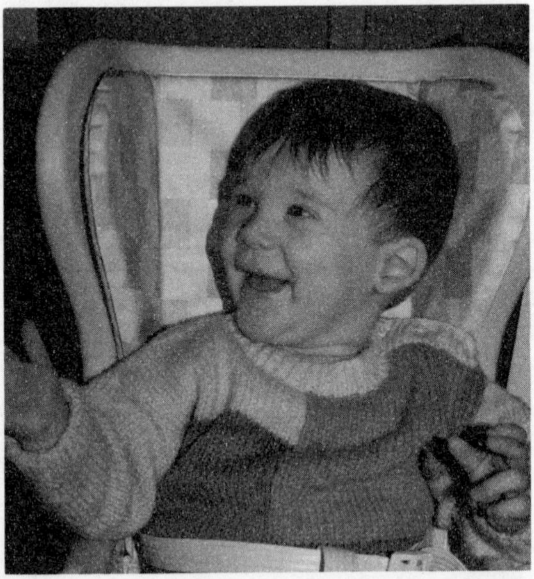	

Figure 3.14 Time: 'Then' and 'Now': What can you see? What are the differences?

Comparing then and now with objects

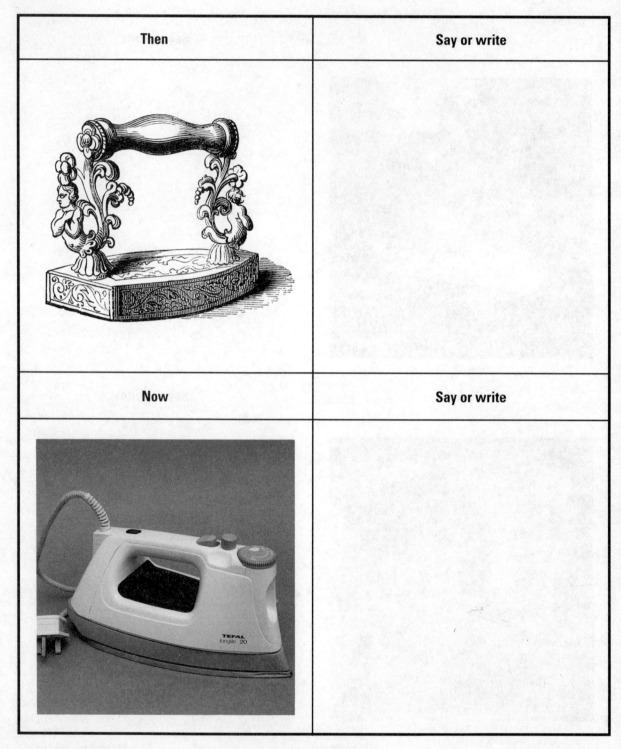

Then	Say or write
Now	Say or write

Figure 3.15 Objects 'then' and 'now': What are they? How are they different?

Sequencing photographs

This is me when I was six months old. My mum is very proud of me.

I am 2 here. It is my birthday.

This is my first day at school.

This is me now.

Sequencing photographs or pictures: A personal timeline

This example is of photographs from their own life, but a progression from this would be to sequence a collection of other pictures as in the next example. Pictures of homes, transport, clothing, lighting, shops are all relevant for sequencing as children have contact with all of these. Younger children will tend to associate black and white photographs with 'old' but you need to talk about this and to get them to look more carefully at what is in the picture and to think again about what they see.

Collect pictures and stories about the bears (see page 38). Discuss these with the children and talk about how making bears has changed. A useful reference book is *In praise of Teddy Bears* by Philippa and Peter Waring (Pictorial Presentations, Souvenir Press). You could also try to arrange a visit to the Teddy Bear Museum at Stratford-upon-Avon.

Another stage in developing a sense of time is to use timelines. These can be started with infants and carried on through key stage 2.

The most successful timeline I have seen and used in classrooms has been a washing line with pegs and cards so that children can hang their pictures or events in the right place whenever they are ready to use the line. At Hatherop School in Gloucestershire, a classroom timeline across the ceiling showed how old the children's houses were, dating back hundreds of years (see below). Each picture of a house said how old the house was (for example, 55 years old) rather than the year in which it was built.

Homes timeline

100 years
ago

Present day

80 years
ago

30 years
ago

70 years
ago

60 years
ago

Example 2: Teddy bear timeline

Looking for evidence locally

The activities described here will help you to meet the requirements of the key stage 1 programme of study:

- Changes in family life and adults around them recently.
- Changes in the way of life of people in the distant past.

Your locality will certainly have evidence for these two elements which children can look at, question and draw.

Looking for evidence of change on an old map (Hatherop School)

Activity One: Our street

Take a series of photographs of different houses or buildings in a street near your school. Include the school building. Try to get a variety of buildings. Give a set of photographs to a group of children (six) and let them have a photograph each. Give out similar sets to the rest of the class. Tell the children that they will be walking along the street and will have to identify their house/building from the photograph and remember its location in the street. Go out for a walk and stop when the children recognise their house or building and ask questions such as:

- Is it an old or new house? How do we know?
- Has it been changed at all (new windows, doors, etc.)?
- What is it made of?
- How big is it?
- What shapes can you see in the house?
- What is next to your house or building?
- If your photograph shows a building other than a house, what is it used for?

When the children come back to the classroom, give each group a basic map of the street on large paper with perhaps one or two clues marked on, for example, the school or trees or a shop. Ask them to talk about where their photograph should be placed on the map and to put them in the right sequence. Then tell them to find the children in the other groups with the same photograph as them and to produce a simple description of their house today, as if they were trying to sell it. You may need to give them an idea of what you mean by describing a house yourself. These descriptions could be wordprocessed or the information put onto a database such as *Our Facts*. The information could all be placed on a street wall map.

Activity Two: Then and now

A second activity is to produce old photographs to compare with the ones you took of your street. You may not be lucky enough to find the whole street but just one photograph will do for discussion.

- How has the building changed?
- Does it have the same use today?
- Is the road outside the same? How has it changed?

A series of photographs of the same building over a period of time would be useful.

Perhaps the school has its own collection for the building or a local family who have lived in the same house for a few generations may lend their family snapshots. Other sources for old photographs will be your local record office or the library where family collections may be housed. The local newspaper office may have good collections as well. If you have access to the census for your street in 1881, you may be able to produce a wall frieze which shows the family changes as well as the changes to the houses then and now. See the picture below.

A wall frieze showing our street in 1881 and now

40

Activity Three: A site visit

From our street, children can visit important local buildings like the church, castles, archaeological sites and discuss what they see there and what it can tell us about how people lived in the past. Divide the children up so each group concentrates on and observes a different part of the building. They need to make drawings, talk about what they see and listen to information about their part of the site so that they can report back to the class in school.

For example, on a visit to a Roman villa, children could be divided into groups which observe and sketch:

- The walls and building materials
- The floors
- The doorways, windows and chimneys
- The living rooms
- The water supply and bathing
- Storage and cooking areas
- The surrounding site.

Back in school, the whole picture can be pieced together from the evidence collected, with the help of pictures and simple guides.

Learning to observe evidence around us is an important skill for history as well as other curriculum areas. Here is a list of features to observe for local work:

- Buildings
- Windows, doors, chimneys
- Road and street names
- House names
- Gravestones
- Street furniture
- Archaeological sites and findings
- Trees and hedges.

Other activities for a site visit include:

- Story-telling in part of the grounds or building, either about an incident or a person connected to the site.
- Searching for clues. The children could be given a sketch or photograph of a clue (part of a building) which they have to find and then answer some questions about the clues. (See page 42.)
- Role-play or dressing up on the site with informed adult direction. There needs to be a purpose to the role-play so try to use education officers or a group like the Young National Trust Theatre Group.
- Observational sketches. Groups of children could be given a room to explore by observing, measuring, asking questions and recording their findings. Cameras are useful here. Back in school the children could present their reports to the rest of the group. (See page 42.)

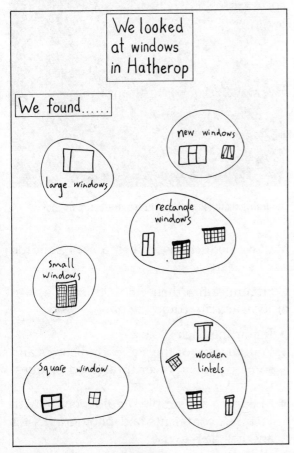

Enquiry work at Hatherop School

- Find the rooms where the people cooked, ate their meals, washed, went to the toilet and stored food. They would need clues for this and a plan or sketch to help them. These questions could be used as a follow up:

  1 How do we know they were used for cooking?
  2 What evidence is left?
  3 How are homes different today?

It is important to remember before asking children to observe, talk about and report to others that they spend time learning these skills in the classroom. Children can be encouraged by simple activities to observe carefully and report clearly. Simple plans of the classroom can be used for hidden objects before you ask them to do this on a site visit.

Children's sketches of their church, Hatherop School

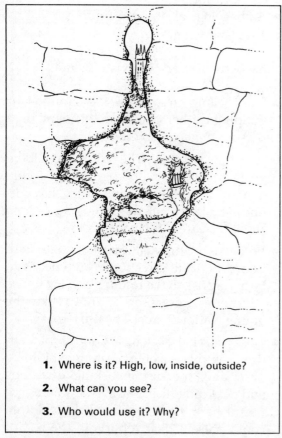

1. Where is it? High, low, inside, outside?

2. What can you see?

3. Who would use it? Why?

A clue from a castle. What is it?

Making deductions is also a skill children need to learn.

Communicating their findings from a visit or local activity could include:

- Reporting back
- Wall display of the site with pictures and some comments wordprocessed or questions
- Making a simple guidebook with pictures, comments and photographs for another class to use
- Writing stories about life on the site in

the past either to tell or to produce as story books with illustrations
- Performing a simple drama in a reconstruction of the site at school. For example, a sheet could be the floor plan for a room in the Roman villa.

The locality is an excellent starting point for children investigating changes. The following aspects could be the focus of the history work over the key stage:

- Homes/buildings
- Shops
- People who help us
- Transport

- Holidays
- Local celebrations.

In dealing with the way of life of people beyond living memory, start with aspects of life children can relate to, such as shops, homes, food, clothing, etc. and make comparisons between then and now. Plan a variety of experiences within a story framework but allow for use of local sites and hands-on activities. Cover the historical content by sharing ideas, research and reporting to each other rather than exposing every child to a similar diet. The diagram shows a range of experiences about Roman way of life.

Tell a simple story based on Romans	To set context and introduce new words, e.g. mosaic, villa, soldier
Making mosaics: paper square or potato prints Give younger children a template to use	
Modelling, e.g. a Roman villa in Lego, or a soldier in playdough	
Finding out about Roman life Research to make a Roman Alphabet	S is for soldier
Handling and drawing artefacts, e.g. Roman coins and pottery	
Writing a story set in Roman times using a wordprocessor and Concept Keyboard overlay	The Chariot Race

Figure 3.20 An activity afternoon on Romans

Using music

At key stage 1, the most relevant musical source is in songs from the different times to be studied. Songs which relate directly to the programme of study for key stage 1 include the following:

> **Britain in grandparents' time**
>
> - 1950s Rock and Roll songs
> - 1960s and 1970s – protest songs such as 'Where have all the flowers gone?' and 'Little boxes'
> - 1960s – Beatles songs, for example 'Yellow Submarine'
> - 1960s to 1990s – songs linked to advertising, for example 'I'd like to teach the world to sing' for Coca-Cola.
> - 1950s to 1990s – Caribbean influences and songs/music linked to other cultures in the community
>
> **Beyond living memory**
>
> - Native American traditional songs
> - Nursery rhymes related to characters or events in history
> - Songs about working life, for example Victorian homes, factories.
> - Medieval songs and madrigals
> - Songs about celebrations and feast days

There are various easily accessible sources for such songs. A & C Black produce a series of spiral bound song books, for example *Songs for Everyone*, which contain examples of the songs suggested. *A Treasury of Children's Songs* edited by Dan Fox (Gollancz, 1989) includes 60 favourites with scores, illustrations and some historical detail for traditional songs, lullabies and nursery rhymes. For teachers planning to look at 'washday' there is the 'Mulberry Bush' with its references to washing and ironing and other chores, for example 'This is the way we iron our clothes'.

Barbara Cass-Beggs, *Musical Calendar of Festivals* is a slightly older publication (1983) but is still available and contains folk songs from around the world related to festivals and feast days. It also celebrates some historical events such as Agincourt, harvest and Independence Day in America with 'America the Beautiful'. There are other references and useful resources such as *This Merry Company 1 and 2* (OUP, 1979 and 1981) by Alison and Michael Bagenal, for their version of a Medieval Christmas as part of a selection of songs from the Middle Ages.

Nursery rhymes prior to the early nineteenth century were songs or melodies sung by adults as well as children and derived from oral traditions. Some rhymes are about characters in history and others about sinister events. Simple examples can be used like 'Old King Cole' to talk about real or fictional characters. 'Dr Foster' is another character who appears in a rhyme with an unfortunate experience in Gloucester. Music advisory teachers would be able to recommend other suitable sources.

Using IT

Children should be given opportunities to use computers for their history work. This may be a simulation in a museum or a simple word processor for reporting their findings. Some data can go on databases. *Our Facts* and *Branch* produced by NCET (Unit 4, Sir William Lyons Road, Coventry) are ideal for key stage 1.

IT can also be used for communicating historical information. Simple word-processing programs like *PENDOWN* or overlays such as *NCET Prompt/Writer* for the Concept Keyboard can actually encourage the use of relevant historical vocabulary and can speed the process of retelling or drafting stories. Booklets of sories can be produced for others to read. The Concept Keyboard with *Touch Explorer Plus* (NCET) also offers the chance to make your own overlays to use with the class, for example a large picture or village map with questions to answer. However, this does involve more input from the teacher.

Planning activities for mixed-aged classes

In some infant schools classes are arranged so that reception to Year 2 children are in the same room. This does mean for history that the teacher has to set up a variety of activities so that children are working at a level relevant to their ability, although the content or topic may be the same. Whilst reception children are making their own personal timelines, Year 1 may be looking at a family history and Year 2 at family life in the past, under a general topic of Families. Year 2 children may cope well with a variety of source material whereas reception may just handle photographs. Progression can be organised so that the same starting point promotes a variety of learning experiences, with activities which increase in difficulty, alongside the use of more source material towards clearly identified targets for each group. Where children work in mixed ability groups the tasks can be identified within the group. Where classes contain one age group, there will still be different ability levels which the teacher will need to recognise in the activities organised.

4

Classroom activities for key stage 2

Study units

The history study units for key stage 2 are meant to provide a balance between in-depth topics, for example, Victorian Britain and broad topics which could look at change over long periods of history, as in local history. Some also give a basic introduction to world history and then focus on a smaller area, for example:

- Romans, Anglo-Saxons and Vikings and focus on one of the above in Britain.

Because the nature of the history units is so varied, activities to develop children's understanding need to be diverse as well as flexible. Within each class there will be children capable of achieving a range of levels at different times during the year. Teachers should plan classroom work aimed at two or three levels of attainment rather than focusing on one level only. For example, with a group of 8–9 year olds, local sources work should allow children to collect information from maps, photographs and building evidence and to make deductions about life at the time studied as well as describing their findings. Or teachers can provide differentiated tasks and direct children towards the most suitable for them. See Figure 4.1. Over the year there should be a combination of these two approaches. For

children with learning difficulties, there may have to be a reduction of content coverage at key stage 2, but the history study units are adaptable enough to allow for some aspects to be experienced by the majority of children. The non-statutory guidance allows schools to base schemes of work on programmes of study for another key stage or to adapt them to individual needs. Some of the ideas suggested in this chapter will be applicable to children with learning difficulties.

At key stage 2 there is more opportunity for children to undertake investigations independently using a range of sources. The DES document states that children should have opportunities to:

" • *Ask questions, choose sources, collect and record information*
- *Select and organise historical information*
- *Present results orally, visually and in writing.*"

(*History in the National Curriculum*, DES 1991, page 17)

Teachers need to plan the history element of topic work so that within each year children have experience of the activities on page 47.

At key stage 2 the issue of content in history becomes more valid, since the programmes of study actually give an outline of the

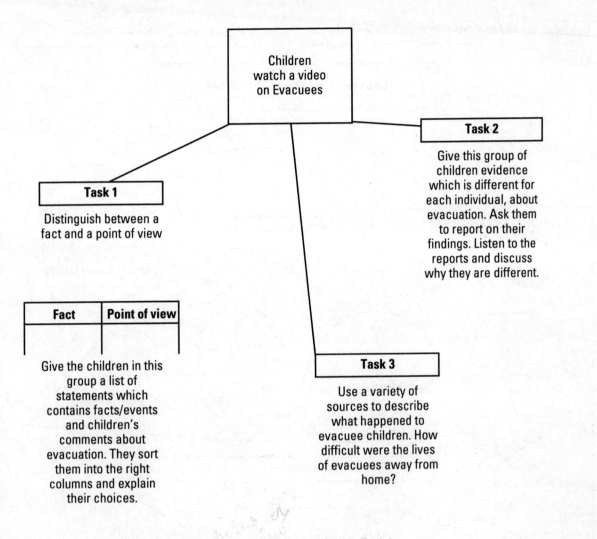

Children
watch a video
on Evacuees

Task 1

Distinguish between a
fact and a point of view

Fact	Point of view

Give the children in this
group a list of
statements which
contains facts/events
and children's
comments about
evacuation. They sort
them into the right
columns and explain
their choices.

Task 2

Give this group of
children evidence
which is different for
each individual, about
evacuation. Ask them
to report on their
findings. Listen to the
reports and discuss
why they are different.

Task 3

Use a variety of
sources to describe
what happened to
evacuee children. How
difficult were the lives
of evacuees away from
home?

All children watch the video and do Task 3

Figure 4.1 Example of devising differentiated tasks linked to the key elements

content areas to be covered for each core unit. Teachers who want similar guidance for the supplementary study units should use the detail in the non-statutory guidance. Although the content is stated with a 'pupils should be taught' proviso, there is complete freedom for the teacher in deciding how this content is to be conveyed. There is no directive to teach in a didactic way or to take children through every aspect as a whole group. In fact, the key elements imply the activities children should be involved in and these are all skills-based and active. A common starting point , such as a schools broadcast on television/ video or an introduction by the teacher for each unit, could then lead into a variety of classroom opportunities which allow children to experience and investigate part of the programme of study and then report back to the class, either in a display or verbal account. The result is that every aspect in the programme of study is dealt with but content coverage does not dominate.

This could be used by children and coloured when they have completed that activity.

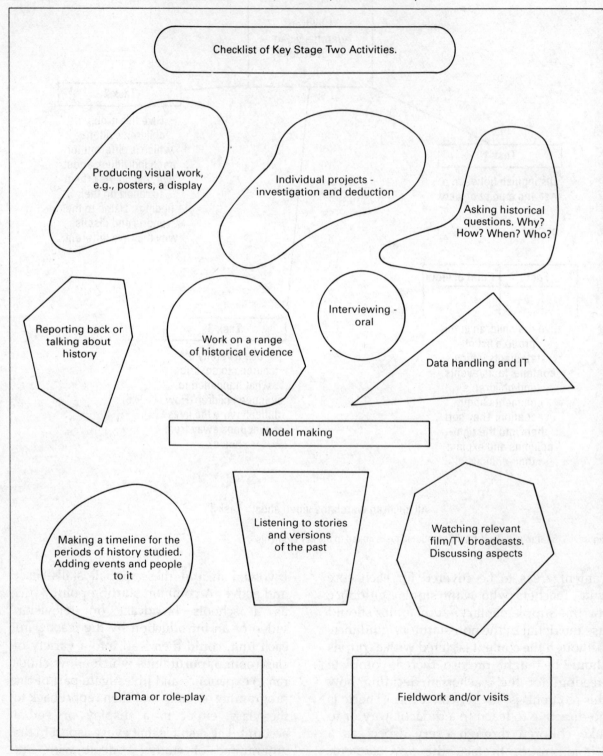

Checklist of Key Stage Two Activities.

Producing visual work, e.g., posters, a display

Individual projects - investigation and deduction

Asking historical questions. Why? How? When? Who?

Reporting back or talking about history

Work on a range of historical evidence

Interviewing - oral

Data handling and IT

Model making

Making a timeline for the periods of history studied. Adding events and people to it

Listening to stories and versions of the past

Watching relevant film/TV broadcasts. Discussing aspects

Drama or role-play

Fieldwork and/or visits

Checklist of key stage 2 activities

Working with the key elements does not mean that the traditional enquiry and project work has to be reduced. However, in the past it may have been communication and presentation skills which were being assessed in projects; now historical understanding and skills need to be considered alongside.

The ideas suggested in the rest of the chapter are generally transferable and open-ended but children in Year 6 should be tackling very different tasks to Year 3 in general, unless they have learning difficulties. Since the choice of when to study the history units remains with the school, teachers will need to check that the tasks suggested are relevant to the ability of children they teach. In a mixed age/ability class, differentiated activities will need to be devised anyway.

Using story

Stories are particularly relevant in history for younger children and when topics such as Ancient Egypt or Ancient Greece are covered in Year 3, the story framework provides an immediate link with the past, for many of the reasons expressed in the previous chapter. In the study unit, Romans, Anglo-Saxons and Vikings, the following stories are useful starting points:

- **Romans** – Myths and legends, for example Romulus and Remus, Aeneas in the Underworld, Hercules, Horatius at the Bridge. Historical fiction such as *A Beacon for the Romans* (Wheaton, 1981) by David Rees; *The Cornerstone* (Heinemann, 1976) by Ruth Marris; extracts only from Rosemary Sutcliff for younger children.
- **Anglo-Saxons** – Beowulf in *Dragonslayer* (Puffin, 1986), *The Lantern Bearers* (OUP, 1959) by Rosemary Sutcliff. See Figure 4.3 on page 50.

- **Vikings** – Norse sagas such as the Creation story or Thor's adventures. Historical fiction such as *The Invaders* by Henry Treece (Brockhampton Press, 1972 available from libraries only) and *The Wind Eye* by Robert Westall (Goodchild, 1986).

For Ancient Greece, studying myths and legends is an important element of study for Greek religion and thought. Children could use a variety of stories and retell them in role-play, picture sequences or scripted drama for older juniors. Good stories which capture the imagination and can be told simply are:

- Theseus and the Minotaur
- The adventures of Odysseus, including the encounter with the Cyclops
- Helen of Troy/The Wooden Horse
- Daedalus and Icarus
- Jason and the Golden Fleece.

For any teacher who continues to study Stuart times, diary extracts make good reading, for example John Evelyn and Samuel Pepys. These can be compared with each other and also other accounts from the time. Children can produce their own diary stories after researching the events, then read them to the class over a few weeks at storytime. Related fiction which is suitable includes Jill Paton Walsh's *A Parcel of Patterns* (Penguin, 1983), about people who suffered the plague through a parcel of patterns sent from London. Also useful is *Children of Winter* (Armada Books, 1986) by Berlie Doherty. Another very simple plague story, *Sentence of Death*, is told at the beginning of *Contemporary Accounts of the Great Plague of London* (Tressell, 1985). This tells how Mary Hoskins discovered her father has the plague and is a good introduction to the topic. This book and its companion, *Great Fire of London*, are excellent sources of contemporary accounts for evidence work with older children. John West has also compiled a series of stories relating to Tudor and Stuart times which appear in *Telltale 3* (Elm Publications, 1990). Each story is backed up by pictures and evidence.

Stories about life in Victorian Britain abound and many teachers will still use Dickens as a source for history. Other useful titles include:

Midnight is a Place, Joan Aiken (Jonathan Cape, 1976), older juniors

Mouldy's Orphan, Gillian Avery (Collins 1978), Year 3/4

Ellen's Birthday, Gillian Avery (Hamish Hamilton, 1971), Year 3/4

Ellen and the Queen, Gillian Avery (Hamish Hamilton, 1971), Year 3/4

The Flither Pickers, Theresa Thomlinson, (Julia McRae Books, 1990), Year 6. (This story is about Victorian Whitby).

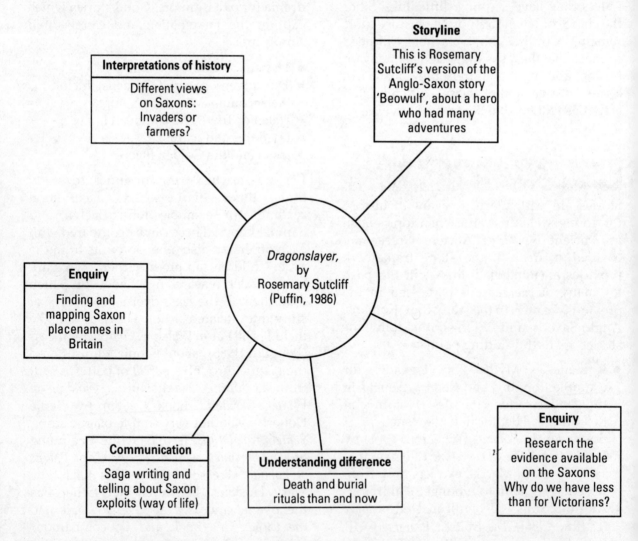

Storyline

This is Rosemary Sutcliff's version of the Anglo-Saxon story 'Beowulf', about a hero who had many adventures

Interpretations of history

Different views on Saxons: Invaders or farmers?

Enquiry

Finding and mapping Saxon placenames in Britain

Dragonslayer, by Rosemary Sutcliff (Puffin, 1986)

Communication

Saga writing and telling about Saxon exploits (way of life)

Understanding difference

Death and burial rituals than and now

Enquiry

Research the evidence available on the Saxons Why do we have less than for Victorians?

Figure 4.3 Link to work on Anglo-Saxons
The story is suitable for older juniors unless told in a simplified form

For Britain since 1930, stories include:
Fireweed, Jill Paton Walsh (Macmillan, 1978)
When the Siren Wailed, Noel Streatfeild (Collins, 1977).

Stories can be a useful planning tool (as with *Dragonslayer*) or as an introduction to the topic. There is a wide variety available which your local library can advise on. The ones suggested here are those I have used successfully in recent years and of course fit with the content we now have to cover. Many good stories are now out of print and are only available through libraries, but with National Curriculum perhaps some of these will be revived and reprinted.

Romans, Anglo-Saxons and Vikings

Boudicca's resistance to the Roman invasion is a gripping story based on limited evidence. As a result, historians have portrayed Boudicca in various ways. Collect a variety of pictures and descriptions so that the children can use them to design their own character sketch from the evidence available.

Preparing for a Roman banquet is always an interesting way of researching the Roman

Boudicca – different viewpoints.

"A very strong woman, calculating and fierce – a warrior but also a woman. Her children made her weak. She was tricked by the Romans. I imagine her as tall, red-haired and strong..."

Books have different descriptions of what Boudicca looked like. Some say her hair was down to her ankles, others to her knees and some to her waist. I have seen pictures of her that are different too.

Jane age 10

way of life. Children would have to investigate customs, clothing, food available, cooking, rooms and members of the household including slaves. Use the A4 pictures or slides produced by Philip Green Educational or postcards from Corinium Museum, Cirencester. For details of Roman food and menus use *Food and Cooking in Roman Britain* (Corinium Museum Publications) by Marian Woodman. See Figures 4.4 and 4.5 (pages 53–4).

Other practical ideas include:

- Making a mosaic with plasticine or printing.
- Studying language and writing techniques; writing with soot and gum; stone work with nails and dental plaster; wax tablets of beeswax.
- Designing and modelling a Roman villa.
- Searching for Roman placenames as evidence (-caster, -ceter, -eter, etc.) to produce a map of settlement.

All these ideas are transferable to Anglo-Saxons and Vikings where the cultural evidence is available.

Life in Tudor times

Produce a booklet of characters from this period. Give children a brief and ask them to produce an A4 sheet on their character as in the example shown in Figure 4.6 on page 55.

Put the sheets together to produce a useful reference booklet for the class.

Using inventories to discover what house interiors were like. Compare these with picture sources. Compare rich and poor. Your local record office will be able to provide seventeenth-century invoices for your children to use. They may be difficult to read, so a transcript would be essential for younger children. A glossary would also be helpful to explain words such as pot hanger, firedogs and irons, and coverlid. An excellent book to use alongside these inventories is *The Blacksmith's House* by Joy James (A & C Black, 1979) which has then and now pictures as well as original sources and explanations.

If you continue to include Stuart times, give children a description of the plague with reasons why it might have happened. Ask them to pick out causes of the plague and produce a diagram with the most important reasons at the top.

Victorian Britain

Since there is so much evidence of the Victorians around us this is an ideal core unit to link with a local study, as in the example for the Forest of Dean (see page 56).

It is also a well-resourced topic in terms of school broadcasts with programmes from *Seeing and Doing*, *Landmarks* and *How we used to live* amongst others which cover content in terms of schools, clothes, homes, culture, work, events and communications. There are also some very good posters, pictures and slides available from Philip Green Educational (112a Alcester Road, Studley, Warwickshire B80 7NR) and Pictorial Charts Education Trust (27 Kirchen Road, London W13 0UD) on aspects of Victorian life, which can be used for 'talking about history' in groups. Teachers could display the posters or pictures and leave question cards nearby for children to answer as an extension activity.

Museums provide interesting hands-on experiences for the Victorian period, detailed more fully in the next chapter, with role-play activities in Victorian homes and schoolrooms as well as handling objects and memorabilia from the time.

Talk about:

From the large pictures or the slides, pick out all the foods which the Romans ate.

Are there any we do not eat today?

Where was the food kept?

What were their dishes like?

Read the card on Roman meals and look at the picture.

What differences can you see? Did they do anything we would not do?

Why do you think they ate differently?

Plan and do:

Use the Roman Recipes card.

Plan a Roman dinner in rough.

Use the Menu cards to make a neat copy.

Add drawings around the card.

Put this on display in your classroom.

Figure 4.4 Roman meals

| YOU ARE INVITED TO A ROMAN DINNER |
| HERE IS THE MENU |

First course

Second course

Sweet course

Made by ....Class ....

Figure 4.5

Name:	**Picture here**
Lived:	
Main reasons for importance	

What historians tell us about him/her:

Your opinion:

Sources used.:

Figure 4.6 Character sketch

IDEAS FOR LOCAL STUDIES IN THE FOREST AREA AT KEY STAGE 2

(These ideas can be related to your own area)

1 Extended walks round the area to observe 'evidence' of the past. Sketching, mapping and recording details.

2 Comparing maps then and now to look at changes, similarities and differences.

3 If linked to the study unit 'Britain since 1930', then local residents can be interviewed or invited into school. Read Winifred Foley's 'A Child in the Forest' (extracts).

4 If linked to 'Victorian Britain', use the local history books which contain people's memories. Some are available from the Library Loan Service.

5 Comparing old photographs of people and places with today. Photographs are produced in two local books published by Alan Sutton or are available from the Record Office or Gloucestershire Collection.

6 Visit sites related to industry in the past, e.g. Clearwell Caves.

7 Use Census material 1851 or 1881 or find out more about local people and occupations in the past. Kelly's directory is also useful for this.

Local archive material is available from the Record Office, Alvin Street, Gloucester.

Evidence of the past - a Victorian school building

Looking at Victorian toys

Children's experiences in the nineteenth century are an illuminating insight for children today and looking at the lives of children through archive material covers many areas of content such as education, public health, religion, culture, families and homes, pastimes, work and crime and punishment. Documents which are available to use are shown in the diagram.

ARCHIVE MATERIAL FOR VICTORIAN BRITAIN

Census 1851, 1881

Trade directories, e.g. Kelly's

School log books (last 50 years closed to the public)

Photographs

Sketches and local histories

School plans

Gaol calendars

Newspapers, including adverts

Sale particulars

Maps

Various activities can be organised around relatively few pieces of evidence. An idea for using census material is shown here as well as a gravestone record sheet.

Children will take great pleasure in linking a gravestone record with a census reference and a photograph of the actual person or the descendants of that person living in the area. Family and portrait photographs can be used by individuals or groups of children to research costume and cultural changes. These questions can be asked:

- Can you describe the costume?

- Who was the person?

- Are there any clues about work or status?

- Why do you think the photograph was taken ?

- How was it taken?

- Compare this photograph with one of a similar person today.

- What does the photograph tell you about him/her?

- What doesn't it tell you?

- Where would you find more information?

Photographs of local scenes also give us clues to the past and how life has changed. You may be able to ask these questions:

- What do you see in the photograph?

- Who do you think produced this photograph and why?

- What are the similarities and differences between this photograph and the scene today?

- What does the photograph tell you about life then?

- What doesn't it tell you ?

Using Victorian sale particulars for a house in your locality allows children to write or draw their comparisons then and now for house interiors and design. Sales particulars are available from the County or City Record Office.

Investigating census materials

What is a census?

Match the words below with one of the descriptions:

Widow   A man whose wife has died
Widower   A person renting a room
Cousin   The person in charge of a household
Lodger   A woman whose husband has died
Visitor   Son or daughter of parent's brother or sister
Head   A person staying at the house

1. **Houses**

   What houses are shown in this census? Try to find them on the old map. Make your own simple map to show where these houses are. Colour the houses which are on the census in 1851.

2. **Occupations**

   Look down the column which says occupations. Make a list of all the jobs people did then. Add the number of people who did that job next to it on the list.

   Use a dictionary to find out about unusual jobs.

   Draw a bar chart on graph paper to show your results. Colour it and label the bars. If you have a computer do this on the database instead.

   What does the chart tell you about jobs then?

   Write a few sentences about it.

   Why did some people have no job written beside them?

   What jobs are not there which people do today? Why?

3. **Family size and homes**

   Look for examples of large families.

   · How many people are in these families?

   Make a list next to their names.

   How big is the largest *household*?

   Choose one of the large families and draw a family tree for them. Write their dates of birth next to their names.

4. Make a map to show where the people moved from, using the column 'where born'.

Place	Name	Relation to Head	Condition	Age M	Age F	Occupation	Place of birth
Hidcote	Martha Dee	Head	Unmarried		38	Grazier?	Ebrington, Glos
	Eliz. Dee	Sister		15		Servant	Mickleton, Warwicks
Ebrington	Joseph Robbins	Head	Married	61		Agricultural labourer	Ebrington, Glos
	Ann Robbins	Wife			40		
	John Robbins	Son		12			
	Eliz. Robbins	Daughter			9		
	Richard Golby	Head	Widower	60		Agricultural labourer	Draycott, Worcs
	Richard Sale	Head	Married	39		Agricultural labourer	Darlingscott, Worcs
	Ann Sale	Wife			32	Agricultural labourer	Ebrington, Glos
	William Sale	Son		14			
	Mary Sale	Daughter			12		
	Sarah A. Sale	Daughter			10		
	Matilda sale	Daughter			8m		
	Charles Cox	Brother-in-law		24		Agricultural labourer	
	William Hobbins	Head	Unmarried	49		Chelsea Pensioner from 68th Foot.	Ebrington, Glos
	Sarah Hobbins	Sister			44	Housekeeper	
	Isaac Hobbins	Brother		31		Agricultural Labourer	
	Ellen Hobbins	Niece			13	Lodger	
Ebrington	Thomas Cox	Head	Married	29		Carter	Ebrington, Glos
	Ann Cox	Wife	Married		25		
	Emma Cox	Daughter			4		
	Mary Cox	Daughter			2	Scholar	

Figure 4.12 Census sheet (1851)

59

GRAVESTONE QUESTIONS

1. What are the measurements of the stone?
Height _____
Width _____

2. Who is buried here?   Age

_____   ____

_____   ____

3. When did he/she/they die?

_____   _____   _____

4. Any other details, e.g., shape, patterns,
verses, stone used, etc. _____

_____

_____

5. Are they on any other document in
school, e.g., census?

The Victorian period also offers the chance to look at changes in domestic objects over 60 years. It was a time of inventions and in many areas of life change was rapid. In other aspects, for example the status of women, little change occurred. Examples are sketched on page 62.

Comparing localities over a long period of time

Another local study unit could focus on change over a long period of time in town and country, to examine the idea of rapid and slow change. This would link well with the geography National Curriculum requirement to look at the locality and the home region, as well as aspects of human geography such as homes, settlement and communication. Within a rural community there is more likely to be evidence in buildings from pre-1600, even from Norman or Saxon times if the church architecture dates from that period.

In fieldwork children can make observational sketches of a variety of buildings and be asked to label them for materials, design, size, description and colour as well as any unusual features. Ask children to look for evidence of change in buildings:

- Windows blocked
- Old arches bricked up
- Changes in materials used
- New windows and doors
- New roof.

Victorian kitchen at the Holst Museum, Cheltenham

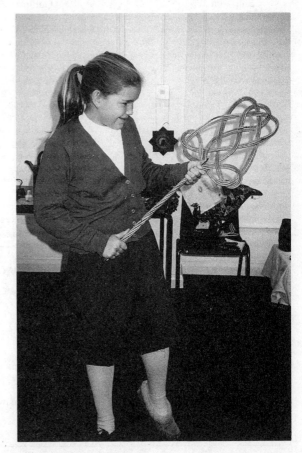

Handling Victorian objects

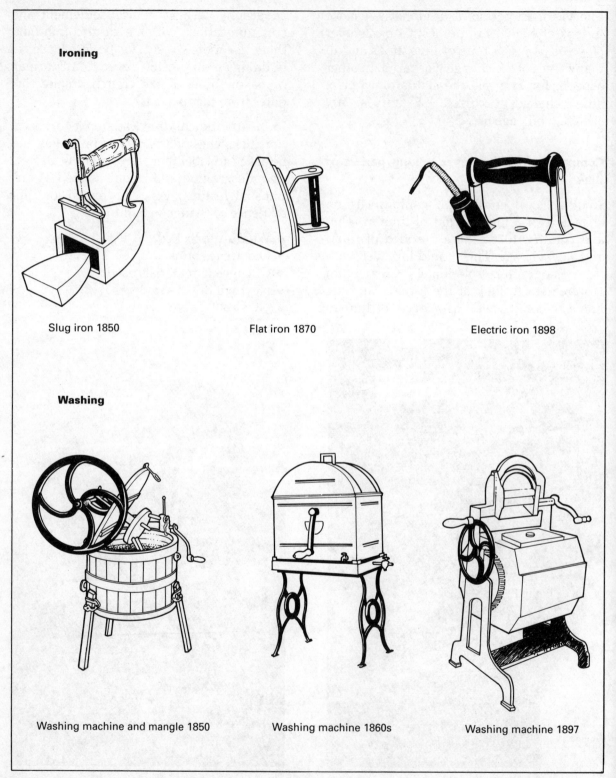

Ironing

Slug iron 1850   Flat iron 1870   Electric iron 1898

Washing

Washing machine and mangle 1850   Washing machine 1860s   Washing machine 1897

Changes in domestic items during Victorian times

Inside the square, sketch a house and use the list of words to label your house:

brick tiles old large terraced stone slates new small detached wood semi-detached cottage house bungalow garden wall tarmac garage chimney plastic.

Add other words if you need them.

Figure 4.15

Colour if you think it helps your picture.
Cut out your house for display.

Link with another school in a different environment so that you have the urban/rural comparison and ask children to compare the two areas by observing the type of houses in each area and counting the number in a defined area. See page 65. This activity combines mathematics and humanities. Children could present the information in bar charts and pie charts using a simple data-handling package on the computer.

Music

Music is a feature of Victorian life for all classes of society. Children could use folk songs and protest songs to link with research into working conditions. Music Hall entertainment and hymns would contrast well and give a flavour of Victorian culture. Musical instruments from the time still exist in homes and museums. Hearing these and using recordings of music helps to create atmosphere for drama and role-play situations. For other ideas related to Victorian life, the resource booklet *Victorian Times* by Jo Lawrie and Paul Noble (Unwin Hyman, 1990) is a treasure trove for teachers. Also use Longman's *Music from the Past*, a series of booklets and tapes for songs from the time. Other Victorian songs can be found in the Cambridge University Press publications, a series of five booklets of songs, ballads and contemporary accounts, for example, *Poverty Knock* about industrial life and *The Painful Plough* about the lives of agricultural labourers.

Older juniors could be given the words from a song to analyse as a source for history and to compare its value against an account on a text or a picture relating to the same issue. In making these judgements the children would be working towards using sources and assessing relative value.

A local study over a long period

With the Revised Orders, there is less opportunity to look at a topic over a long period of time, but the Local History study unit could still be used for this. Timelines around or across the classroom can still be created with published materials or children's own work.

One idea to try is a timeline of 'inside and outside houses' which encourages the children to research as well as to identify where their house should go on the timeline. I have used this activity with eight year olds after sequencing and discussing pictures of houses and buildings through time. They should encourage children to talk about style and building materials. Children are presented with a photocopied drawing of the outside of a house which they have to identify. They then have to find out about the interior and draw or label the inside of the paper. See the example given on page 66. The drawing shows how this can be done for a Victorian house.

Once the drawings are complete they can be placed on a timeline which the children devise and then each group reports on their home from Roman to Viking to Medieval to Tudor to Regency to Victorian and today.

The above activity is a starting point from which the children could identify local examples of their pictures. Comparing then and now, using pictures or photographs as in the example shown on page 68, is the extension activity which could also lead into a comparison of then, then and now, for example Roman, Victorian and today.

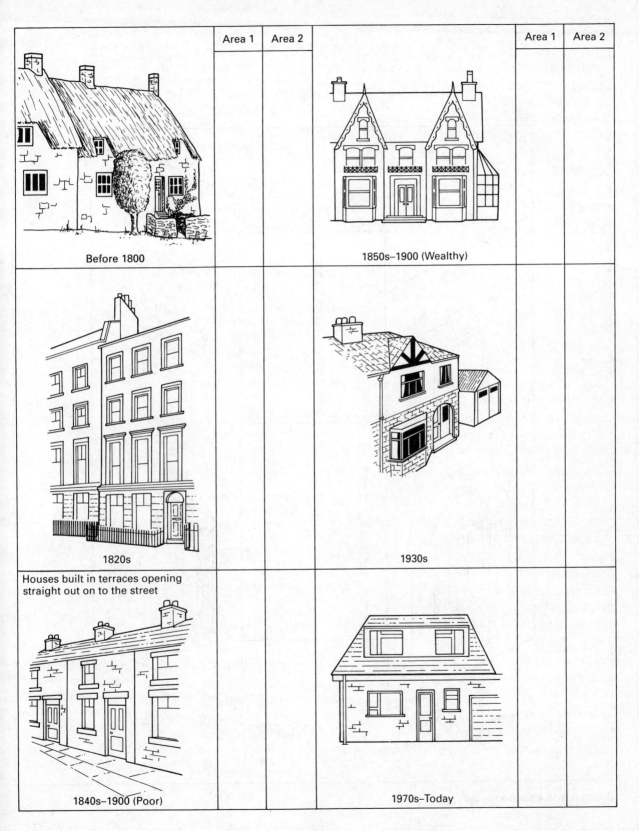

	Area 1	Area 2			Area 1	Area 2
Before 1800			1850s–1900 (Wealthy)			
1820s			1930s			
Houses built in terraces opening straight out on to the street						
1840s–1900 (Poor)			1970s–Today			

Outside/Inside a Victorian house

COMPARING 1900 AND NOW

Look at pictures A and B.

1 Give a title to both pictures.

2 Put an approximate date on the rooms in the pictures.

3 List the activities which you can see in the 2 pictures.

4 List 5 objects which you can see in each picture. Are any the same? Why or why not?

5 Why does the room in A appear more untidy than in B?

6 Which room would you prefer to live in? Give your reasons.

7 Which of the two ladies in the pictures do you think has the easiest life? Say why.

8 List all the changes you can think of in the home which would explain the differences between the two pictures.

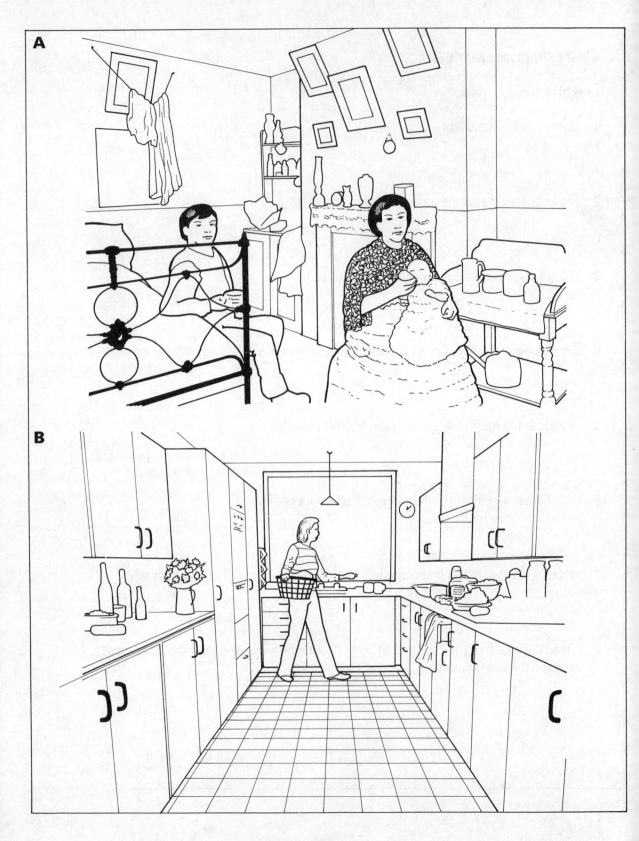

Britain since the 1930s

This unit is likely to be covered by older juniors so I will start with activities relevant to them.

- Collect a series of comments and brief accounts about life during the Second World War. Try to collect material suitable for a variety of readers. Divide the statements up in to positive and negative, then give groups only positive or only negative statements. Ask them to read the items, then write a news item based on what they have read. When they have finished, the groups could read out their news items and discuss why they are different.
- Re-enact an evacuation from school. Read evacuees' letters and diaries as well as secondary sources. Collect memorabilia from the time and invite local people into school to talk about their memories. Tape record them and discuss why oral history may be unreliable evidence. Look at photographs to discover cultural changes since the 1930s.
- Design a questionnaire for parents and grandparents to find out about changes since 1930.
- Set up research groups to look at inventions, industry, transport. Use local evidence and examples. Visit a factory today and compare with pictures from 30 years ago. The factory may be able to provide photographs.

For younger juniors the following activities may be more suitable:

- Listen to an evacuee story and produce a picture sequence with subtitles to show what happened. Explain why children had to be evacuated.
- Handle and try on a gas mask. Why was it needed? Draw a poster to warn children about why they should carry their gas masks all the time.
- Look at newspaper pictures from the time about bombing and air raid shelters (*Picture Post* has been reprinted recently). Talk about how families would cope. What would you take in the shelter? Children could then write a diary extract using the pictures and other available evidence.
- Make a ration meal or set out a week's rations and compare with a shopping basket today. Discuss how food and packaging have changed.

A Non-European society

Although this title for the unit is rather Eurocentric, I think it is one of the few opportunities children have to study another culture from its own perspective and also in terms of its archaeological remains. One of the choices is the Maya, a civilisation in Yucatan, Mexico which was rediscovered by explorers in the eighteenth century. These people are mainly remembered for their pyramid-style stone buildings and unusual arches. Archaeological evidence includes a variety of stone buildings, murals depicting Mayan culture, their calendar and religious beliefs. Since a site visit to see the evidence would be unlikely, children would need to learn about the Maya from pictures and descriptions written by archaeologists and historians.

Maya AD 250–900

Start the topic by brainstorming on 'what we want to know about the Maya'; see page 70.

- Use pictures and information on clue cards. Give different questions to groups of children and ask them to find out as much as possible from the clues they have and to report back.

Mayan civilisation

- After the reporting session, look at how many questions were left unanswered. Talk about how historians and archaeologists fill the gaps in the evidence.
- Recreate a Mayan city as a frieze or model from the evidence.
- Compare Mayan mathematical skills, astronomy and calendars with ours today.
- Compare Mayan road construction with Roman and today.

Using IT at key stage 2

There are more IT packages available for key stage 2 than for key stage 1. Children should be able to gain experience of the following during the key stage:

- Using databases to store and retrieve information and also answer historical questions and test ideas.
- Using simulations to help historical understanding.
- Using word processing and desktop publishing as a means of communicating historical information in news reports for example.

The following packages exist, but do not all link with study units; most of them contain information booklets as well as programs:

1665 The Great Plague (Tressell, 1987)
Into the Unknown (Tressell, 1985)
Exploration and Encounters (Tressell, 1991)
Viking England (Fernleaf, 1984) see worksheet on page 72
Placenames – database on KEY (ITA/GSN Educational Software)
Census – database on KEY (ITA/GSN Educational Software)
How we used to live 1874–1887 (YTV)

The Concept Keyboard mentioned in the previous chapter can be used successfully with juniors and the NCET package, *Touch Explorer Plus*, comes with two suitable programs for the history units: *Elizabethan Cottage* and *Time Tunnel* (a street 1874–1988).

Teachers can design their own overlays for any of the history units.

Databases for key stage 2 which are more demanding and versatile than those mentioned previously include *GRASS* and *KEY*. These are usually available from your LEA on licence or from your IT advisory teachers who may be able to recommend other simple data-handling packages. Databases which will produce information in bar charts and pie charts are particularly useful when handling census information.

Using drama and role-play

Whole school drama days are often very effective as the culmination of a topic. *The Inspector Calls* could be a Victorian schoolroom with a visiting School Inspector (an adviser, a governor or local resident). Costumes are essential to give the day authenticity and children can be organised to take part in drill, spelling tests, reciting tables and practising handwriting.

Another idea is a Roman banquet, already mentioned in this chapter, or a scene from the Fire of London. There are numerous possibilities but the important thing to remember is that any role-play needs to be informed and should come at the end of research so that children's understanding is enhanced by the experience.

A simpler activity to organise can be based on artefacts, enquiry and reporting as shown in the example described by Robert on pages 73–6.

Objects can be borrowed from a local museum and used in context for simple

My Viking raid

I am a Viking. My name is...

I am going on a raid to the English coast. I have been chosen as the leader for this voyage. I will have to decide where to land.

If I return home the Council will judge me on how many prisoners I bring back and how much money and riches I have taken.

Figure 4.19 Worksheet for Viking England

Drama with artefacts

3 boys in a group :

The activity set for this lesson was to report back to the class, about our objects in any form that we wished, be it a role-play, or just straightforward talking.

Our group decided to do a short sketch, showing how the various pieces of equipment were used around the time that they were made.

We went about this by first doing a short piece of improvisation, after discussing what our basic storyline was going to be, and who the three characters were going to be played by. After this we sat down and wrote the script, after some more talking among ourselves to fix the final storyline. Here it is:

Characters- 1 Bodysnatcher.
             2 Policemen.

It is a dark night, and a gravestone can just be made out. Near it the bodysnatcher is frantically digging, hoping to get the body before he is caught. But he is too late; two policemen come in, shining the lantern cautiously. They go down two separate paths, and catch the criminal red-handed. After a struggle, he is put into handcuffs, and led off to jail.

As they go along, the policemen tell the bodysnatcher exactly what is going to happen to him. When they reach their destination, the man panics but the police are merciless, for they sit him down in a chair and put his thumbs in the thumbscrew, until the criminal confesses who put him onto the job. As they release the cruel form of torture, he hastily goes back on what he said. However tightly the policemen screw up the thumbscrew, he refuses to tell the truth, so the two take him away to be locked up.

◯   these are artefacts used
in the drama.

WHAT I LEARNT

Doing the role-play helped me to understand better, the early police force coped with criminals. It was also more exciting than just reading about the objects because, however well a book describes something, it is never quite the same as holding it, seeing how big it is, it's texture, it's colour, and shape. It is also wonderful to be able to look at it   in any way you like, and to see the care and precision that was put into these very beautiful items from the past.

My group had the following five objects, each relating to law and order :

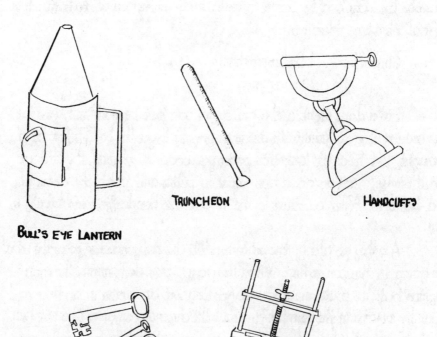

BULL'S EYE LANTERN   TRUNCHEON   HANDCUFFS

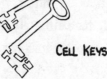

CELL KEYS   THUMB SCREW

We had to identify the object, guess at when it was made and who it was made by, who used it, what it was used for, and why we thought that particular object had survived, along with some other questions.

Here is an example.

(I have turned the original isolated answers into a piece of writing, to make it more interesting to read).

OBJECT: <u>Bulls eye lantern.</u>

DESCRIPTION: So called because its front lens is shaped like an eye, (see picture on previous page), so as to throw the light out more. It would have been used by the police, or Bow Street Runners, as they were called, and before those, by night watchmen.

It is made of tin and glass, and might have been made by a whitesmith, a person who specialises in making things with tin, like lanterns. It would have survived because people might have wanted to compare it with outdoor lighting in the future.

Its modern equivalent, is, of course, the torch.

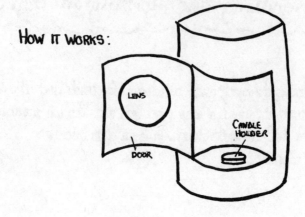

HOW IT WORKS:

1. Open door.
2. Put candle in candle-holder.
3. Light candle.
4. Close door.

Over the past week we, in groups, have been studying household emplements, washing utensils and other things as a preview to our new project, MACHINES.

This is to describe what we did in each of the three lessons, and also to say what I learnt from the piece of work.

Lesson 1.

We were divided into groups, and given a number of objects, each with the same basic 'theme'.

role-plays which are researched before performance to the class so that wherever possible the children's comments are not anachronistic. If possible, use a video camera so that you can discuss the reports and pick up any points of concern or ones you wish to expand on in general discussion. Drama of any sort needs time to plan and execute.

Teachers should not try to include these ideas in too many topics to the detriment of other concepts and skills in history.

IT and drama are two forms of communication in history. I'll finish this chapter with another – poetry, from Laura, aged 9, who tells us what she thinks history is.

What is history?

History is what happened long ago
Like Victoria's reign and jubilee
And family trees that grow and grow.
All the rats that caused the plague
Smelly sewers-
Those horrible chewers.
Romans fought to win their battles
Poor farmers feeding all their cattle.
Roman feasts,
Roman priests,
Stone straight roads
For sandals with open toes.
Soft togas,
Legendary ogres.
Knight fighting dragons
Wooden horse-drawn wagons.
People in the stocks
Black market selling pots.
Jesus, born at Christmas time.
Christmas songs all in rhyme.
Heads chopped off in the French revolution,
But now, history will be all this terrible pollution.

Laura, aged 9
Christchurch School, Cheltenham

5

Museums and history teaching

"*Museums... properly interpreted and used, have an enormous potential for bringing history to life and creating a lasting impression on pupils.*"

(*History for ages 5 to 16* DES 1990, page 178)

Museums now provide a wide range of activities, mostly on the premises but ranging from observation to active involvement in role-play. To begin we will look at the services on offer inside the museums and how schools are and should be using them. Later in the chapter we will look at using museums in the school.

"*These activities all contribute to broadening the range of historical evidence considered by pupils, in ways that engage all the senses and encourage exciting and imaginative work.*"

(op.cit., page 178)

Below are listed the benefits which children should gain following from a museum visit for history.

Key stage 1

- The ability to handle and observe objects as well as drawing them
- The ability to ask questions about objects and find answers by handling them
- The ability to classify objects
- A relationship with museum staff so that they understand and appreciate their role and work.

Key stage 2

- Children should have visited a variety of museums and made comparisons
- They should be able to ask and answer questions based on the museum
- They should be able to keep up their interest for the visit and observe over a longer time period
- They should be able to record their observations in a variety of ways
- They should be able to talk about the role of the museum and its purpose, as well as making suggestions for improving displays and presentation.

Observational drawings of artefacts at Cheltenham Museum

Visiting a museum will probably link to part of the key stage 1 programme of study or to a study unit at key stage 2. It also fulfils many of the requirements for looking at and making deductions from sources for history. For example:

KS1 Holst Museum, Cheltenham	
Role-play in the Victorian kitchen and laundry	Communicate information acquired from a source, e.g. a kitchen utensil – explain how it works
	Ask and answer questions using sources. What was life like for a laundry maid?
KS2 Visit to Corinium Museum, Cirencester	
Study Unit Romans; Anglo-Saxons and Vikings in Britain	Make deductions from sources (about Roman life)
	Put together information from a variety of sources, e.g. produce a booklet on Roman technology after a museum visit

Figure 5.1 Links between museums and history skills

Preparation

More than ever now, a museum visit needs to be clearly linked to the Curriculum so that the objective for the visit is clear to the teacher and children. With infants you will need to choose museums within easy travelling distance and with a majority of hands-on activities.

- Decide how the museum visit can extend your classroom experience.
- Visit the museum yourself and liaise with museum staff on access, facilities, costs, supervision, etc. If the museum officers are talking to the children or arranging an activity, then they need to pitch it at the right level.
- Use information and work/quiz sheets from the museum only if they suit your needs. Remember that these are provided for everyone who visits the museum and may not be geared to your topic or ability range.
- Ask about back-up materials which can be used before and after the visit, for example, slides, artefacts.
- Try to involve the children in an activity at the museum, for example, handling artefacts or role-play, since this will help them to remember.
- Try to set up problem-solving questions for children to research rather than simply 'find out about' or copy or describe what they see. For example:

'How do we know what a Roman villa looked like? Find the evidence and note it down.'

- Allow time for observational sketches and for children to choose to look at an area or an object they particularly enjoyed.
- Prepare your helpers so that they know what the children are supposed to do and why.
- If you have disabled children, check that the museum is suitable and can provide the facilities you need.
- You may wish to use picture books as an introduction to a first museum visit. The following are available:
Packed Lunch for the Museum, Steve Eales (Mantra)
Me and Alice go to the Museum, Paul Rogers (Bodley Head)
My Class Visits a Museum, Vivien Griffiths (Franklin Watts)
Let's go to the Museum, Janine Arnos (Cherrytree Books).

Museums with an archaeologist: A mock dig

Children can dig down through reconstructed layers to find items like the ones on display in the museum as well as recognisable modern items in the top layer. This will give children an idea of the work of the archaeologist plus an awareness of the gaps in our evidence of the past.

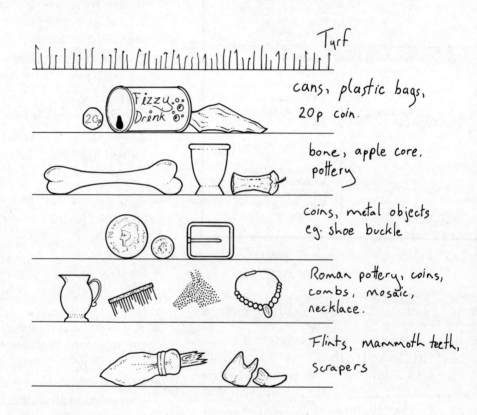

Turf

cans, plastic bags, 20p coin.

bone, apple core, pottery

coins, metal objects eg. shoe buckle

Roman pottery, coins, combs, mosaic, necklace.

Flints, mammoth teeth, scrapers

An operational dig

Experience of work in an excavation site or an area in the school/museum grounds can be very useful. Archaeologists or education officers can help children to classify and label their finds. These could be recorded on a simple database or displayed as part of a classroom museum.

Use Education officers in museums for the following.

Handling artefacts and role-play

Many museums now provide opportunities for children to handle objects in a classroom at the museum. Some can provide workshop activities as well but the teacher always needs to check that these are relevant to the children and link with the school follow-up.

Role-play is offered at some specialist museums. At the Grosvenor Museum in Chester, children have the opportunity to dress in replica Roman uniform and think about the problems which the soldiers would face, for example coping with the extremes of weather whilst marching from place to place. A similar opportunity can occasionally be set up by groups such as the Ermin Street Guard and the Sealed Knot, although these tend to be more difficult to arrange. Members of the Ermin Street Guard have regularly spent a day or two at Corinium Museum in Cirencester so that children have access to them there.

At the Black Country Museum in Dudley, children can 'leg' their way through a tunnel as part of a canal boat ride and can wear Edwardian costume in the photographer's parlour. At the Beamish Open Air Museum, there are opportunities for the children to dress in 1920s clothing and take a particular role from the period, such as a shopkeeper, and to work in that role for the afternoon. There is a 1920s town complex as the historical setting.

The City and Folk Museums in Gloucester provide opportunities for children to experience life in the Roman city of Glevum, with Roman foods, coins, costume, pots and wax writing tablets. See page 82.

They also provide a Victorian schoolroom activity in the Bishop Hooper School (which is part of the museum) with drills, hymns, slate boards, ink dipper pens and spelling tests as well as mock punishment. The Holst Museum in Cheltenham provides opportunities for a Victorian Kitchen and Laundry experience which can be geared towards infants, juniors, including children with learning difficulties.

Blists Hill Open Air Museum at Ironbridge can offer primary children a morning in a squatter cottage and Tollhouse on the site, to dress in period costume and work as children might have done in Victorian times on daily chores. Wiltshire have set up their own Victorian schoolroom in an authentic setting at Sevington and have discovered many original artefacts to use with the children, including a child's reading book from the time. Copies of this have been reprinted and are available to purchase.

Time boxes

Rather than looking at artefacts from one time period, some museums are now offering a box of selected items for handling to use in sequencing and discussing changes over time. Some boxes like Derbyshire Museum Services 'Blue Box' contain cue cards with prompt questions for the artefacts, such as 'Is it authentic or a replica?' The Cheltenham Museum offers a similar service to primary schools as a loan box. These boxes encourage schools to put their own time box together. Children enjoy this experience and it is useful reinforcement of the museum activity.

Rubbings

Rubbings can sometimes be made of artefacts as well as asking children to do observational drawings. The National Waterways Museum at Gloucester Docks offers a variety of workshop activities in the

A taste of life
in
Viroconium

step back~
in time

REMEMBER

School

Parties

Welcome

THE
ROMAN EXPERIENCE

Children will be provided with Roman costume (not sandals) and will be able to handle genuine Roman artefacts and use replicas in role-play situations.

Sample lessons using wax writing tablets, weighing with a steelyard, coins, pots, armour and more.

Special treat – an opportunity to sample Roman food!!!

Recreating the feel of Victorian costume and mood

Dolly and washtub at the Holst Museum, Cheltenham

schoolroom but also the opportunity to work on large cast metal signposts from the canal era to make rubbings and take these back to display and discuss in the classroom.

Computer simulation

Again the National Waterways Museum, amongst others, encourages visitors to use the interactive computer simulation of the workings of a lock gate. This is an activity which is beyond the resources of the average school and often is a great attraction with children. Other museums also use computers as part of their learning experience.

Videos

In all museums you will find information boards and other visual display material but many are now introducing short video films to evoke an atmosphere or explain a development in the museum. Because these are aimed at a general audience the teacher may need to interpret and direct the children to particular sections. The Roman Museum at Bath has a good example of a video film explaining aspects of the display.

Films and photographic evidence

Museums such as the Imperial War Museum provide opportunities for children to see archive film relevant to their studies. The National Museum of Photography, Film and Television at Bradford offers various workshop opportunities in their studios, as well as the Museum of Moving Images in London. Teachers will need to make sure the material and activities are relevant and that there has been adequate preparation work in looking at images for history beforehand.

Portraits

The National Portrait Gallery offers a wide range of famous people of different kinds and cultures for children to study and in some cases a variety of images of those personalities. This is an interesting aspect of history because you can introduce children to the idea of different artistic interpretations as a source for history, but also use the pictures as evidence of home life, culture and clothing. Postcards are on sale of various portraits and these are a very useful and cheap classroom resource, for fol-low-up work.

English Heritage have produced two very useful teacher's booklets, *Using portraits* and *Learning about objects*, with plenty of classroom ideas which would link with a museum visit.

Skills and concepts

What skills and concepts are you trying to develop through museum work?

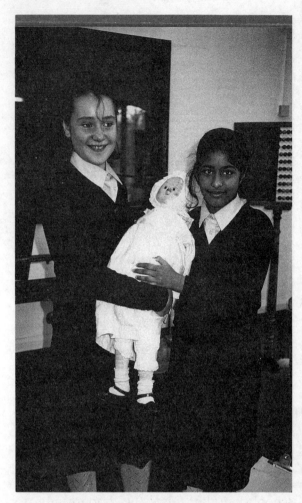

Girls from St John's School, Cheltenham handling old toys

Skills	Concepts
• Enquiry/research	• Similarity and difference
• Observation	• The nature of evidence
• Oracy	• Sense of time
• Literacy	• Interpretations of history
• Empathy	• Change and continuity
• Interpersonal skills through groupwork and co-operation	• Are you fostering particular attitudes as well?
• Recording and reporting – communication	• Enthusiasm/enjoyment
• Synthesis/making deductions	• Appreciation of value
• Handling skills	• Curiosity
• Problem-solving	• Confidence
• Data-handling	• Awareness
	• Caring and conserving

Follow up work

Back in the classroom, the teacher can channel the enthusiasm from the visit into further investigative work, reinforcement of handling skills and observational drawings using artefacts or slides/pictures, display work and presentations. Children's work will be more purposeful and directed if there is a specific objective and audience, for example:

- A school assembly presentation
- A booklet/guide to the museum for another class
- A display for parents.

Allow for differentiated activities in providing a range of resources in the classroom. For example, Census material and Trade directories can be used by children as a follow up to a Victorian museum so that they identify their experiences with real people in the locality. See the section on Census work in Chapter 4. Pictures/photographs from the nineteenth century can be organised for others to use.

Key stage 1 work from visits can be planned around reconstructing aspects of the museum in the classroom, for example:

- Objects in clay
- Models of buildings
- Sketches of artefacts
- Larger reconstructions, like a kitchen or parlour
- Making mosaics after a Roman visit
- Recreating sounds from the past and story-telling
- Singing songs from the time
- Handling objects
- Looking for evidence from the locality
- Making a time capsule to bury in the school grounds.

KS1 Museums	
TOYS/ CHILDHOOD	Bethnal Green Museum of Childhood, London Teddy Bear Museum, Stratford-on-Avon Cumberland Toy and Model Museum, Cockermouth Museum of Childhood, Sudbury, Derbys Vintage Toy and Train Museum, Sidmouth Ethnic Doll and Toy Museum, Kent Museum of Childhood, Ribchester, Lancs Doll Museum, Warwick
HOMES	Avoncroft Museum of Buildings, Bromsgrove Ironbridge Gorge Museum, Telford Black Country Museum, Dudley
VICTORIANS	Gustav Holst Museum, Cheltenham St Fagans Museum, S. Glamorgan
See KS2 grid for TRANSPORT	
KS2 Roman	Lunt Roman Fort (Reconstruction), Coventry Grosvenor Museum, Chester Corinium Museum, Cirencester Verulamium Museum, St Albans Roman Baths Museum, Bath
Viking	Jorvik Viking Centre, York
Ancient Greece, Ancient Egypt	The Greek Museum, Newcastle upon Tyne British Museum, London Horniman Museum, London Ashmolean Museum, Oxford Ulster Museum, Belfast
Life in Tudor Times (plus Stuart Times)	(The Cromwell Museum, Huntingdon) Mary Rose Ship, Hull and Exhibition, Portsmouth Shakespeare Globe Museum, London Geffrye Museum, London (The Museum of London 'Great Fire experience') Speke Hall, Merseyside St Fagans, S. Glamorgan Mary Queen of Scots House, Jedburgh

Figure 5.2 Museums related to study units

Life in Victorian Britain	Quarry Bank Mill, Styal Ironbridge Gorge and Blists Hill Museum, Telford Osborne House, Isle of Wight National Waterways Museum, Gloucester Chatterley Whitfield Mining Museum, Black Country Museum, Dudley Beamish Open Air Museum, Co. Durham
Life since 1930 in Britain	Imperial War Museum, London Eden Camp, Malton, N. Yorks.
Aspects of Local Naval History	Portsmouth Naval Museum and Base Maritime Heritage Centre, Bristol The Boat Museum, Ellesmere Port. Captain Cook Birthplace Museum, Middlesbrough Exeter Maritime Museum National Maritime Museum, Greenwich Chatham Historic dockyard, Kent
Aspects of Local Transport	National Motor Museum, Beaulieu Heritage Motor Museum, Brentford York Railway Museum Didcot Railway Centre, Didcot Surrey Heath Museum, Camberley Museum of British Road Transport, Coventry

can never be a substitute for a museum visit but offers a valuable alternative. Again the children need preparation so that they are handling and questioning for a purpose and to gain most from the exercise.

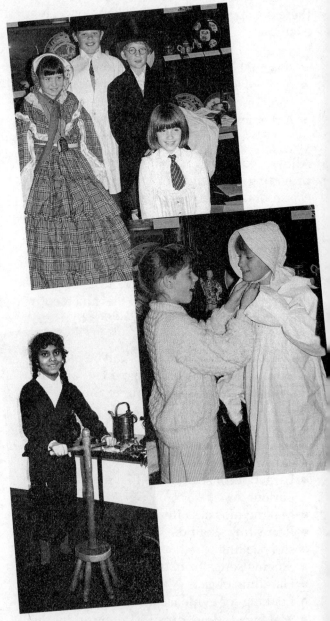

Gloucestershire pupils enjoy the experiences offered by the Cheltenham Museum

Museum staff in your classroom

Charging policies often make extended trips, involving the cost of coaches, difficult to fund for some schools. Occasionally a local museum will provide a service with their education officers which brings aspects of the museum to you. Look out for sessions which can be linked to your programmes of study or related to the locality. There may be a charge for this, but it will be less than taking all the children to the museum. This

What do we class as museums today?

Teachers will find a wide variety in the services and facilities available to them. Some museums may not even welcome an invasion of schoolchildren on a regular basis. These museums may be the ones that are private collections with limited access or those whose philosophy is one of collection and conservation, not public display.

Teachers need to look at the literature carefully and decide which museums cater for their specific needs. At the same time, there are new centres opening which bear little resemblance to the traditional halls of well-labelled display cases and prefer to call themselves Heritage Centres. There are well over 50 of these in the country and more appear each year in towns which are on the tourist routes. The Oxford Story and York Story are examples. They are much more of a business venture than a museum and more of a theatre than a presentation of historical artefacts. They are aimed at adult tourists and families rather than educational links with schools. Children enjoy the experience they offer, but teachers need to realise exactly the kind of interpretation of history they are digesting.

For the Teacher

1   How does the museum fit with your topic? (starting point, reinforcing a classroom idea, extra stimulus)

2   What specific activities do you want the children to experience? List them and talk to the museum staff when you book the visit.

3   Plan what they will do, observer and record. Make worksheets if relevant.

4   Inform parents/collect money/ check transport and insurance, etc.

5   Inform and prepare the children.

6   Organise helpers. Do they know what to do?

7   Work towards the visit in the classroom, making sure that children have practised the skills they will need.

8   Tell the children what their final objective will be in terms of display/presentation

9   Enjoy the day. Invite museum staff to see your work/do a follow up.

10   After the visit, get the children to send letters to the museum.

11   Evaluate the exercise and list any observations soon after the visit. File your notes for next time or the next teacher

---

Figure 5.3 A museum checklist and planning sheet for the teacher

6

Teacher assessment and recording achievement

Purpose

Assessment of children's progress in history and reporting to parents is now a legal obligation for teachers but there are other relevant reasons why we should monitor children's achievement. In primary schools, teachers need to make daily assessments of their children's progress to set suitable tasks for the next day/week. These may well be instinctive reactions, based on good practice over years, rather than formal intrusions in to classroom activities, but they have been taking place for many years without causing too much trepidation or disruption of learning. National Curriculum assessment may be seen as an imposition but it merely formalises a process which has been in existence for a long time in many schools. Most teachers would not argue about the need for monitoring progress. One major purpose of assessment for the government is to inform on standards against level descriptors for core and foundation subjects; history is one of these.

Teachers monitor children's progress through assessment for sound educational reasons rather than accountability, and make decisions about future activities as a result. There is also the opportunity to check whether the objectives planned for that topic have actually been achieved. If not, they need to be considered again. These two purposes are particularly useful if the class is moving on to another teacher who will need to know what they are capable of achieving in history and what tasks had been set for them in the previous class.

Headteachers may view assessment as a means of checking that National Curriculum areas have been covered and how skills and understanding are developing in their school. It will also be a check on standards between schools, which may not be welcome since all assessments need to be placed in context and one school will have very different criteria to the next, for example, in terms of catchment. This more sinister purpose of National Curriculum assessment seems to imply that schools will be compared with each other in a league table approach. Wherever possible the assessments need to remain in the hands of the teachers so that the purpose continues to be more than a legal obligation and a mechanism for reporting to parents.

For history, a child's historical under-standing can never be measured fully by a series of activities and tests. The Revised Orders provide a more acceptable framework for monitoring progress.

The level descriptors provide an overview of key characteristics of children's work at each level. These are provided for end of key stage judgements. The key elements have been set out clearly to give a framework for planning and on-going assessment. If teachers have planned history activities linked to key elements and allowed for the progression shown in these, such activities will produce the evidence of pupil attainment. Assessment under the Revised Orders is much clearer and linked to the learning objectives in the key elements.

Practical solutions

Since there are no SATs for history at primary level, the assessment decisions are firmly in the hands of the school and LEA.

"… assessment should be based entirely on teachers' own judgements of pupils' classroom work, although informed, as teachers see fit, by the use of non-mandatory tests…"
(Education Reform Act 1988, Section 4 Order, *History DES Circular 4/91*, 1991)

The materials provided for the non-mandatory tasks in history at key stage 1 were felt to be well-produced and continue to be useful resources. Teachers have already integrated these ideas into their work and may well continue to use similar ideas for assessing students in history. On a day-to-day basis and to inform planning, the key elements need to be used alongside the content of the revised study units. Feedback to children on their progress should be linked to the learning objectives of the key elements.

In primary schools assessments are generally formative anyway, preferring an on-going developmental approach rather than an end-on test. Teachers should aim to make assessments for history in a variety of ways:

- Informal observation during classroom activities
- Talking to children about their work and planning their work
- Assessing the products of children's activities, for example, displays, drawings, booklets, answers, etc.
- Discussing work assessed by the child or a group of children.

Observations can be made during:

- The visit of a speaker or story-teller – watch the children and take note of good questions or answers
- Individual enquiry into an aspect of the topic
- Groupwork on a presentation/exhibition
- A visit to a museum or historic building/ site
- Local fieldwork.

Throughout the learning process for history, children will progress and regress against the statements in the key elements, which form learning objectives. This is why repetition of activities is essential to reinforce the concepts and allow for children's performance to benefit from work being presented in a variety of ways, some of which will be more relevant and motivating to the individual than others. Assessment evidence can be gathered from marking work, from listening to 'pupil-talk' and from observing. At the end of the key stage, this evidence should be compared with the new level descriptors and used to provide a 'best fit' description for each pupil. It is very important to have a range of evidence from each pupil before comparisons are made with level descriptors. This evidence, possibly a folder of work and teacher comments, needs to be from work based around the key elements and the required content to allow teachers to make judgements more easily.

Devising tasks

Your tasks for assessment need to vary between open-ended ones. Use the flow diagram and examples to help you plan.

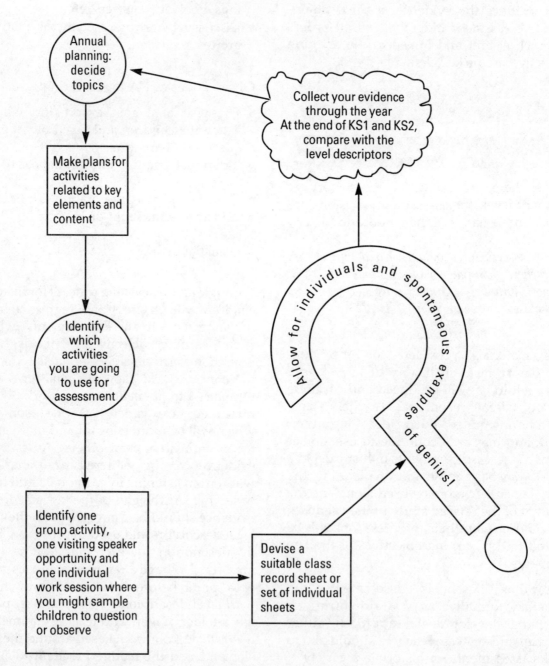

Figure 6.1 Planning for assessment

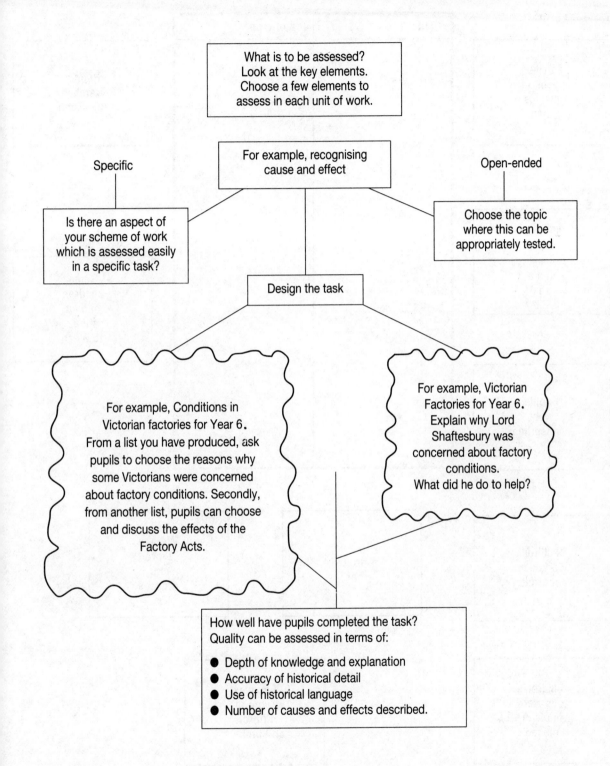

What is to be assessed?
Look at the key elements.
Choose a few elements to
assess in each unit of work.

Specific

For example, recognising
cause and effect

Open-ended

Is there an aspect of
your scheme of work
which is assessed easily
in a specific task?

Choose the topic
where this can be
appropriately tested.

Design the task

For example, Conditions in
Victorian factories for Year 6.
From a list you have produced, ask
pupils to choose the reasons why
some Victorians were concerned
about factory conditions. Secondly,
from another list, pupils can choose
and discuss the effects of the
Factory Acts.

For example, Victorian
Factories for Year 6.
Explain why Lord
Shaftesbury was
concerned about factory
conditions.
What did he do to help?

How well have pupils completed the task?
Quality can be assessed in terms of:

● Depth of knowledge and explanation
● Accuracy of historical detail
● Use of historical language
● Number of causes and effects described.

Figure 6.2 Devising tasks which can be assessments

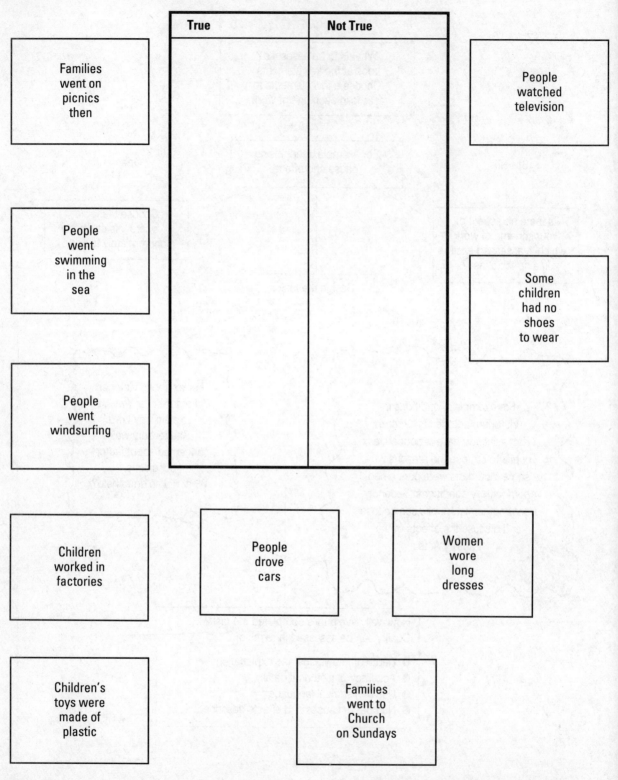

True	Not True

Families went on picnics then

People watched television

People went swimming in the sea

Some children had no shoes to wear

People went windsurfing

Children worked in factories

People drove cars

Women wore long dresses

Children's toys were made of plastic

Families went to Church on Sundays

Figure 6.3 Assessment activity in life in Victorian times: KS1

Based on an idea from Elmlea Infants School

Bedrooms at Three Points in History

An activity to assess knowledge and understanding at KS2

17th century

Great Chamber: A Chest of Drawers, Table & Stand ---00J:0:0

A Bed furniture & Bedstead - - - - - -002:15:0

From an inventory 1690

19th century

Tent bedstead and mattress
Feather bed, bolster, and pillow
Two sheets, 4 blankets, & 2 counterpanes
Mahogany chest of 5 drawers
Carpet, hearth rug, and 2 mats
Washstand and ware, chair, & towel horse
Painted table and glass
Half-tester maple bedstead & straw mattress

Feather bed, bolster and pillow
Carpet and hearth rug
Maple-painted washstand and ware
Dressing table and towel horse
Mahogany dressing glass
Large bookcase, glass front, and cupboard
   under
Holy Bible, 2 vols

From a sale catalogue 1881

Today

List the items in your bedroom today. Then compare the three bedrooms and describe how and why they have changed over 300 years. Present your findings in a variety of ways.

The true-false activity for infants on page 92 is open-ended and would allow you to intervene and ask further questions, whereas the inventory activity for juniors is more specific to looking at change over time.

After seeing pictures and listening to stories related to the statements in the chart, children are asked to place in the correct column each of the cards. Make the chart larger and laminate it along with the statement cards. Children can be asked why they have placed the cards in a particular column. They should be able to refer to evidence in the photographs/postcards in the classroom or the stories they have heard.

Activities suggested in Chapters 3 and 4 can be used for assessments.

Monitoring procedures

Discussing examples of children's work with other teachers can be a time consuming exercise. But until we feel comfortable with learning objectives and what they mean in history, we will need to consult each other, at least informally during the key stage so that any reports on progress are well-informed and standardised. If two teachers share a year group as two classes, then as part of planning time could be allocated for looking at children's work and comparing opinions on attainment. Alternative a session in an In-service day could be set aside to do the same, possibly with advisory help.

It is important to look for specific historical attainment in children's work as described in the key elements. Children can produce good descriptions which are relevant, but may not show evidence of such concepts as 'cause and effect' and 'difference'. This is why setting the appropriate assessment task is vital.

In small schools where there may not be enough staff to have a viable discussion on children's work, an alternative would be to use the local cluster of schools and hold an annual discussion or display of work on a topic. This could be a chance to look at each other's ideas as well as resources and assessment. Where there are still LEA advisory staff, history specialists can offer professional input on assessment and monitoring school progress.

Recording achievement

"*... to build up a record of evidence of each pupil's attainments, which may include examples of work as a basis for future judgements about the levels reached at the end of the key stage.*"

(*DES Circular 4/91*, page 7)

A record of progress/achievement is on-going and should include the following:

- Children's attainment in history
- The study units covered by the teachers with visits and fieldwork noted
- Any coverage of cross-curricular aspects within the history topics, for example, IT, the Multicultural dimension and Economic and Industrial Understanding (EIU).

Examples which teachers might like to adapt for their own school are on pages 95–6. History record-keeping should be in line with the school policy for other subjects and should mean the minimum amount of work for the individual teacher. Attach topic plans to records to save writing out the tasks set again. If planning is done thoroughly then the assessment and record-keeping will be more straightforward.

Key elements	Teacher's notes on progress and tasks completed

1 Chronology
  a) Sequencing objects and events
  b) Using the language of time	

2 Range and depth of historical
  knowledge and understanding
  a) Remembering what happened
  b) Recognising cause and effect
  c) Identifying differences	

3 Identifying different ways the past is shown	

4 Enquiry
  a) Looking at different sources
  b) Asking and answering questions	

5 Communicating history, e.g. telling, drawing and writing	

Name .... Teachers ....

....

Figure 6.4 Individual record of progress for history, key stage 1

Name	Teachers ....
Date of birth..	....

Key elements	Teacher's notes on progress and tasks completed
1 Chronology a) Making timelines b) Using dates, time language and understanding periods in history	
2 Knowledge and understanding a) Describing features of periods and societies b) Explaining reasons for and results of events c) Making links between aspects of history	
3 Explaining why there are different interpretations of history	
4 Enquiry a) Using a range of sources b) Asking and answering questions c) Selecting and recording relevant detail	
5 Communication a) Recalling information b) Using historical language c) Using various ways to retell history	

Figure 6.5 Individual record of progress for history, key stage 2

7

Evaluation and review

Refer to the planning diagram in Chapter 2.

Evaluation is an on-going process both for the individual teacher and for the school. At certain times though, an in-depth review of history provision within the school needs to take place. This could be linked to a formal process such as an OFSTED inspection or to an In-service day on history for all staff. The co-ordinator and headteacher need to set areas for review and have clear ideas about objectives. The review may be introduced by a simple questionnaire to teachers so that areas of concern are highlighted and as much information as possible is available. Wherever possible the questionnaire should be anonymous.

The results of the survey can be analysed and the main areas of concern pin-pointed for discussion at the staff meeting or on a training day. Prior to the discussion or as

Answer the questions below by circling the most relevant score on the right.

	Poor	Average			Excellent
1 Resources for history in the school are . . .	0	1	2	3	4
2 Staff expertise in history is . . .	0	1	2	3	4
3 Implementation of NC history has been . . .	0	1	2	3	4
4 The co-ordinator's contribution to school history is . . .	0	1	2	3	4
5 Understanding and trialling of assessment needs in history is . . .	0	1	2	3	4
6 School visits and organisation of fieldwork is . . .	0	1	2	3	4
7 Progression in activities for history is . . .	0	1	2	3	4
8 The use of outside help and advice for history is . . .	0	1	2	3	4
Our major success in history is					
Our major weakness in history is					

Figure 7.1 Survey related to history in Good Practice Primary School

part of it, a target sheet could be produced with suggestions of how to improve a particular area. For example, if the area of weakness appears to be resources (marked 1 on the 0–4 scale), how can the school remedy this so that the score in a year's time would be three or four on the same scale?

After the discussion, set dates and allocate the responsibility directly to members of staff, probably the co-ordinator and librarian. Some of the areas of concern identified may need outside help, so look for people in the LEA or elsewhere who could come along, or for courses which staff could

Staff Room Notice Board

<u>Improving history resources</u>

Please write below any suggestions for improvement.......

Parents to catalogue pictures and posters.

More money to spend.

A resource area in the library.

Buy reference books for teachers.

Swopping ideas more between teachers.

Boxed resources for history topics.

Join up with local schools and share resources.

Ask the adviser to come with examples.

Keep children's booklets as information for the next year.

More variety. Some computer programs as well.

For discussion at the next staff meeting.

go on which would improve confidence and skills in history teaching. Often an evaluation will highlight problems which take a long time to solve either because there are financial constraints or because there are factors beyond the control of the individual school. This does not mean that raising these issues is pointless, but in recognising the problem the school may set long-term targets over five years and seek outside help to achieve their objectives. It also makes the matter clearer for the Governing Body and other interested parties.

The evaluation may be on a much more informal level from year to year at the annual planning stage.

- How did this year's topic choices work for history?
- Did we cover political, economic, religious, social and cultural aspects in key stage 2 overall?
- How do we move on from these topics for next year?
- What aspects need emphasising now with each class?
- How have new children to the school fitted into the middle of key stage 2?
- How have our assessment plans worked?

The answers to these questions will define what happens for the next year and what new ideas might be tried. When evaluating topic plans, try to incorporate children's evaluations of the topic or the activities they were engaged in. Highlight activities which were motivating and others which failed to stimulate and then analyse why. For example, were they too difficult, too repetitive, content dull, and so on? Of course, some classes will react differently to the same material, but you may see the activities from a different perspective simply by asking the children to contribute their ideas. Whether formal or informal, the evaluation process is fundamental to sharing the

implementation of National Curriculum history in schools, to supporting colleagues and spreading expertise. The conclusions after evaluation may well alter original planning for schemes of work and choice of history units. These aspects of the school's history policy should be seen as flexible since many areas of the school may change over the next few years. For example:

- School population
- Intake quality
- Staffing
- Buildings
- Curriculum content.

Long term planning which has the evaluation built into the process can help a school develop in other areas. History cannot be the focus of discussion in such depth every year, but an on-going programme of review for all subjects will allow staff to be objective about their achievements and concerns. It is a positive approach to coping with new initiatives and allows school finances to be allocated in a balanced and pre-planned way. A formal evaluation focus might look like this for a five-year cycle.

Year	Main focus
1	History and Geography
2	Science and IT/Technology
3	Whole school issue, e.g. building
4	English and Maths
5	Creative areas of the Curriculum

NB   Other issues will be evaluated each year but the above items are major ones.

Classroom teacher

On an individual basis, teacher appraisal will form part of the evaluation process. It may be that during an appraisal interview, the teacher has an opportunity to talk about areas of specialism as well as training needs. The appraiser, probably the headteacher, will need to suggest how teachers can improve their understanding of history, personal knowledge and teaching techniques if necessary. This may be through advisory help in the classroom, in-house training or an extended course at a local college. Look for mini-projects in your LEA where you can bid for funding to develop a curriculum area with advisory help. There may also be expertise within your local cluster of primary schools which you can tap to help an individual or group of staff. Also think of new ways of using INSET time so that one or two teachers can have time out of the classroom to research and plan topics or visits for history. It is optimistic to think that expertise is acquired overnight when so many new initiatives have to be integrated into the primary curriculum, but confidence and reassurance can go a long way in helping the classroom teacher to deal with history concepts and content.

The co-ordinator

In Chapter 1, the role of the co-ordinator for history is dealt with in detail. Alongside other teaching roles, it may appear to be an impossible task, but as with whole-school evaluation, if realistic targets are set for each year then the job becomes manageable and more satisfying. The co-ordinator will discuss the tasks allocated as part of the appraisal system and prior to the interview, needs to have noted the areas of achievement for the previous year. The tasks set out in Chapter 1 might be a useful checklist if there is no clear job description. Each year a different aspect of the role could be highlighted. For example:

Year 1 – Revision of schemes of work in the light of the latest orders

Year 2 – Resources audit to improve quality, storage and access

Year 3 – Staff training and evaluation of the new schemes of work

Year 4 – Check on progression and assessment

Year 5 – Review and update policy documents

HMI reports on Humanities teaching in primary schools have emphasised the importance of the co-ordinator in making history provision effective. Choosing the right person for the job is the first step and providing regular support and acknowledgement could be the key to the successful implementation of National Curriculum history throughout the school. Regular and systematic evaluation puts history firmly on the curriculum map and enhances the role of the co-ordinator.

Keyword Index

Also available in this series

Really Practical Guides

This series is designed to provide primary teachers with up-to-date, accessible guides to good primary practice in line with the demands of the National Curriculum.

Titles include:

The Really Practical Guide to Primary Assessment, Second Edition — Wendy and David Clemson

The Really Practical Guide to Primary RE, Second Edition — Hubert Smith

The Really Practical Guide to National Curriculum 5–11 — Wendy and David Clemson

The Really Practical Guide to Primary Science, Second Edition — Carol Holland and John Rowan

The Really Practical Guide to Technology — Ron Adams and Peter Sellwood

The Really Practical Guide to Primary Geography, Second Edition — Marcia Foley and Jan Janikoun

Books can be purchased over the telephone by credit card, and information obtained on 01242 228888, fax 01242 221914.

The Really Practical Guide to Primary Assessment, Second Edition

David and Wendy Clemson

A readable and friendly guide to assessment that explains what primary school teachers, staffs and governors need to know – and how to put it into action.

- what the real issues are
- what the National Curriculum demands
- how to master the jargon of assessment
- how to make sensible choices for teacher-based assessments
- how to carry it out effectively (and stay sane!)
- how to compile practical and useful records and reports
- how to cope with the pressures of time and from parents
- how to manage assessments at school and class level
- how assessment can help you improve children's learning

A special practical workshop section provides a complete INSET package of lively and positive activities for you and your staff to use together.

What the *TES* said about this book:

"Refreshing … highly readable … the assessment requirements of the National Curriculum are clearly explained … together with anything else a primary teacher is ever likely to want to know about assessment … a guide to how to go about assessment and what to do with the results."

The Really Practical Guide to Technology

Ron Adams and Peter Sellwood

This book covers all aspects of primary design and technology and provides a large bank of practical lesson ideas. The first part explains how to prepare schemes of work, organise, record and assess primary technology. This is followed by a substantial ideas bank of topics for use in the classroom and a comprehensive, illustrated guide to components, materials and tools. The ideas throughout are linked to the requirements of National Curriculum.

The Really Practical Guide to National Curriculum 5–11
Wendy and David Clemson

A thought-provoking, readable book to help you develop your teaching further – both individually and across the whole school

The Really Practical Guide to National Curriculum 5–11, highly praised by the *TES*, is a professional guide to better teaching and learning in primary schools

It covers:

- the issues and how to explain them to parents
- better National Curriculum planning
- teaching through subjects and topics
- how to develop better teaching strategies
- how to manage National Curriculum more effectively
- how to tackle evaluation
- how to cope with change
- an action plan for looking at your present work and improving it – at both class and school level.

What the *TES* said about this book:

"Clear ... concise ... original ... dynamic ... uncompromising ... down-to-earth."

The Really Practical Guide to Primary RE, Second Edition
Hubert Smith

An invaluable and up-to-date guide to planning and teaching RE in the 1990s. It explains what the law now says about teaching RE in school, what the aims of primary RE should be, how to plan an effective RE programme and how to deliver it in the classroom. Throughout, attention in given to managing RE alongside National Curriculum demands and there are special sections on assessment and resources.